They're Only Words

They're Only Words

by
Mark Levy

with illustrations by
Brian Belanger

Belanger Books
2019

They're Only Words
© 2019 by Mark Levy

Mark Levy can be reached at:
creativeLEVY@gmail.com

For information contact:
Belanger Books, LLC
61 Theresa Ct.
Manchester, NH 03103

derrick@belangerbooks.com
www.belangerbooks.com

Cover and Design by Brian Belanger
www.belangerbooks.com
www.redbubble.com/people/zhahadun
www.zhahadun.wixsite.com/221b

To Arlene

I can never disappoint
the person who loves and
believes in me so much.

Foreword

In 2007, your humble broadcaster received a letter and selection of essays from a patent attorney in Binghamton, New York, where the local public station, WSKG, carries *Weekend Radio*. The subjects were varied, wry personal histories, comment on social conventions, musings. These were not belly laugh causing, but resulting in smiles and nods of recognition. His name is Mark Levy, and he was told that *Weekend Radio* was interested, but the features needed to be shorter — about three to four minutes — and his pay would be local and national recognition and glory, and maybe a Tortuga Rum Cake at holiday time. So, now in the year of our Lord 2019, The Wisdom of Mark Levy continues on *Weekend Radio*, rotating with the two other radio essayists. Mark moved his base of operations, first to Boynton Beach, Florida and then to Evergreen, Colorado. There, he, on occasion, retires to a deep, dark, damp writers cave and creates a half year or so of features at one sitting, essays with such varied titles as "Building Insult Vocabularies," "My First Puppy," and "Back to Basics — Roman Numerals." He then records the material for shipping off to WCLV. He has a daughter in Cleveland, whom he visits periodically, and visits WCLV. And Mark does receive a Tortuga Rum Cake, or sometimes a Racine Kringle, at holiday time as thanks for another year of witty and wry commentaries that don't necessarily cause belly laughs, but smiles and perhaps, nods of recognition.

Robert Conrad, President
WCLV

Cleveland Orchestra Broadcast Service
Host: *Weekend Radio*

Preface

I used to go to bed thinking about obscure things, like "why don't we still use Roman numerals to calculate?" and "what's the difference between a bibliophile and a bibliomaniac?" and "if I had the money, what's the most expensive thing I could buy?" I used to hope to remember the questions the next morning so I could look up the answers in my local library. But now with the Internet, I don't have to wait until the next morning and I don't have to find the answers in obscure books. I can get them almost immediately at my computer or my cell phone. I can access just about all the information in the world by touching or even talking into my phone. Pretty cool.

It occurred to me that if I wanted answers to these types of admittedly silly questions, maybe other people did, too. Then I found a quirky radio show called *Weekend Radio* on the Public Radio network. It had a sprinkling of classical music, comedy albums — many being British — and audio essays.

"Hey," thought I, "I wonder if there's a place on that show for me to share my questions and observations?"

So I recorded a couple of my essays on CDs and mailed them to the producer of that show in Cleveland, Ohio: Robert Conrad. He thought they were interesting or foolish enough to broadcast and the rest is history. I also funneled some of my essays in written form to the Mensa Bulletin and to an impressive but little-known online magazine called ragazine.cc.

What I hadn't bargained for was a constant need for more material. Fortunately, I shared the weekly broadcast with two other essayists, so the pieces I recorded myself aired only tri-weekly. As it turned out, that wasn't a problem for me, since I think of many, many new questions within those three weeks. The Internet helps me research answers and sometimes moves me in unexpected directions.

Since the essays in this book were written for audio taping and radio broadcast on Weekend Radio, you may see certain references to the show or to Robert Conrad. You may even see some pronunciation hints for the narrator (me). Feel free to ignore them or, better yet, imagine you're listening to me read them.

This is the second volume of my essays, the first group appearing in **Trophy Envy**, available on the Amazon site and, as they say, wherever fine books are sold.

Mark Levy
Evergreen, Colorado

Contents

TECHNOBABBLE

STRANGE OBSERVATIONS

THEY'RE ONLY WORDS

Am I Being Too Literal?

The word "literal," for me, has gone from being mildly annoying to exasperating. After you hear why, I am pretty sure it will literally rankle you, too.

Literal is an adjective that means taking a word in its usual, explicit, or most basic or ordinary sense. When you're being literal, you're about as straightforward as you can get. So, if you say "the temperature is literally freezing," it means the temperature is no greater than 32 degrees. And if something "literally takes your breath away," it means you can't breathe. That's literal.

The opposite of literal is *figurative*. A figurative word or phrase is more imaginative or abstract. One type of figurative language is metaphorical, a figure of speech which is a way of understanding complex ideas via familiar idioms. An example is "I work like a dog," or "I can hear my mother-in-law snoring a mile away." Those phrases are not literal, since I normally can't hear her snoring from the other side of my house.

I have two problems with the way the word "literal" is used nowadays by broadcast news reporters and commentators. The first misuse is placing it in an obvious way that doesn't even require the "literal" word.

I recently heard a weather person on T.V. say, "it's literally sleeting here in Boston." I think the message would have been perfectly accurate and a bit shorter if she had said, "it's sleeting." No one would interpret the word, "sleeting" any other way than sleeting... frozen ice pellets falling from the sky. Even if she hadn't said "literally," I would have understood the sleet to be literal.

Another weather person exclaimed that much of the Midwest was "literally in the single digits." Couldn't he have made that statement without saying "literally?"

Maybe I'm watching the Weather Channel too much, but weather people seem to use the word in this redundant sense more often than anyone else. Of course, others do it, too.

A newscaster, speaking about the infamous character, Jihadi John, expressed his opinion that the FBI was conducting a "literal ongoing investigation." I mean, what other sort of ongoing investigation could the FBI conduct? If FBI personnel engaged in metaphorical investigations, I wouldn't be the only one to accuse them of being overpaid.

The way I see it, to use the adjective "literal" to modify a noun that has no other meaning is a literal waste of time.

But more disturbing is when a person inappropriately says "literal" in a situation that is clearly not literal. For example, "literally raining cats and dogs" can't happen unless a hot air balloon carrying a load of pets loses its wicker basket.

I recently heard a newscaster state that Congress was "literally hanging onto Benjamin Netanyahu's words." Unless his words were suspended from the underside of a bridge and the members of Congress had, well, literally steel grips, those folks could not literally hang onto Bibi's words.

So many people use the word "literal" inappropriately, I can hardly get through a day without being affronted by somebody's language. Maybe my skin is literally too thin.

I've tried to be diplomatic in correcting everyone at every chance I get, including talking back to the T.V. But I've noticed that my comments are often considered obnoxious, didactic, and/or critical. At the rate I'm losing friends, the entire problem may disappear, as no one will want to talk with me. And that would be a shame because I literally have so much wisdom to share.

I hate to remove words from the dictionary, but I think this word should be on the top of the endangered lexicography list. Its use is either inappropriate or redundant. Either way, there's about as much need for it as literal hen's teeth.

A New Word

William Shakespeare added 1,100 words and phrases to the English language all by himself. That's an incredible literary accomplishment. He gave us "whirligig" and "buzzer" and "wild goose chase."

It's hard to contribute a word of the same caliber as "luggage," for example, but I think I've invented one. It's actually a combination of two popular exclamations that leaves one with the distinct impression of both of its parents.

I know by now you're incredibly curious. I won't keep you in suspense any longer. Ready? Hope you're sitting down. It's... **YEKES!**, a combination of *eek* and *yikes*.

YEKES! has a somewhat more sinister flavor than *yikes*, which is a neutral word defined as "an interjection that expresses mild shock or surprise." *Eek*, of course, is an exclamation connoting not only surprise, but also revulsion, repulsion, or horror, like when a mouse suddenly appears in the kitchen.

My new word, *YEKES!*, means "Wow, that's a crazy thing and pretty scary, too." I would use *YEKES!* to express a reaction to a terrible accident involving a living being.

For instance, if I saw an innocent puppy lose its tail, "Yekes!" I would exclaim. People would immediately know the importance of the occasion and its horrific dimensions, even before they knew the details thereof.

Seeing a young man with his tongue frozen to a metal light pole and knowing part of his tongue would have to be removed, would elicit *YEKES!* from me. It's comforting to know what to say in that situation, which happens more than you'd think and almost always to a young man, not to a mature man or to a woman of any age.

And just like *eek* and *yikes*, the word *YEKES!* would always demand an exclamation point. I wouldn't say or write *YEKES!* casually. There's a certain degree of urgency in suddenly exclaiming *YEKES!* and nothing but an exclamation point will do.

Now *YEKES!* is way too strong a word to describe mundane situations such as witnessing the fiery crash of a drone aircraft. Mechanical events and accidents like that don't rise to the level of a *YEKES!* incident. Nor would a minor mishap, like a hair in my soup or someone's finger being stapled, justify a *YEKES!*

Basically nothing short of decapitation or at least amputation of a major limb accompanied by copious blood flow would result in a *YEKES!* I'm concerned that the overuse of *YEKES!* could dilute the gravity of the word. If I say *YEKES!* when I notice a typo on a menu, what would I have left to acknowledge significant mayhem?

According to yellowpages.com, only one person in the United States is named Yekes and yellowpages.com states the most common given name for that surname — I would argue in this case it's the only name — is Evelyn. She lives in Illinois. This seems to be an appropriate time to shout out to her. Coincidentally, I had a beloved aunt named Evelyn who also lived in Illinois. What is it about that state that attracts Evelyns?

But I digress. It's true that my word *YEKES!* will not be used as often as, say, "gosh" or "heck," but I'll settle for my minor contribution to be associated with and complement Shakespeare's "set my teeth on edge."

Bibliophile or Bibliomaniac?

A fine line exists between genius and insanity. As a book collector, I've discovered a fine line exists between *bibliophiles* — those of us who love to read and collect books — and *bibliomaniacs* — people who are obsessed with collecting them. Sometimes bibliomaniacs are referred to as biblioholics, as opposed to bibliotaphs — people who hide or bury their books, or bibliokeptomaniacs — those who steal books, or biblioclasts — those who destroy books. The affliction of bibliomania has been called a gentle madness.

Really, isn't it just a matter of degree if you own 5 books or 50,000? I like to think so, but maybe I'm too close to the subject.

One of the groups of books I collect deals with case studies of bibliomaniacs. The descriptions of those crazy people allow me to feel more normal. I get the same feeling of normalcy, by the way, when I watch The Jerry Springer Show. I tell myself I'm not that bad. I'm clearly more normal than those other folks, I tell myself.

In the early 1800s, a fellow named Richard Heber had acquired close to 200,000 books in his 60-year lifetime. He said no gentleman can be without three copies of a book — one for show, one for use, and one for borrowers. Heber needed more than his modest home to store them all. In fact, he bought eight houses to store them, some in England, some on the Continent. Well, I've only got one home, and although it's packed to the gills with books, and yes, from time to time I've considered building an addition, I've never thought of purchasing another house, much less seven more of them. So I'm not as bad as Mr. Heber... yet.

Another collector had so many books, he couldn't fit a mattress in his home, so he slept standing up. I'm certainly not that bad... yet.

In the 1830s, a former Spanish monk who kept a library at a monastery was so enamored with books that he committed at least eight murders in the course of stealing part of the victims' libraries. Personally, I've received all of my books lawfully, as gifts or by purchasing them. I wouldn't consider stealing a book or murdering my fellow bibliomaniacs — I mean bibliophiles. I'm just not that bad... yet.

I do have one regret. Understanding, as I do, that I have the collector's gene in me, perhaps a collection of any items would have satisfied me. Let's face it: books take up a lot of space, more than postage stamps but less than automobiles. Jay Leno's 130 cars and 93 motorcycles take up a lot more room than my paltry book collection, I often tell my wife. But she reminds me that my whole collection of thousands of books could probably fit on a single e-book.

If I had the opportunity to start over at the age of nine, I would have started collecting fine jewelry, a miniscule piece at a time. Elizabeth Taylor's collection of jewelry was sold at Christie's Auction House in 2011. The two-day sale of 270 lots realized a staggering $137.2 million for her jewelry. One of her pieces was called La Peregrina, a 16th century pearl necklace, which sold for $11,842,500. I like to think I could have acquired the equivalent piece eventually by buying one pearl at a time.

The Duchess of Windsor, formerly known as Wallis Simpson, had a collection of more than 300 pieces, worth $50,300,000. Frankly, I've never been a fan of hers. And in my opinion, all those jewels didn't make her look anywhere near as gorgeous as Kim Basinger in her prime. But I don't mean to be catty. After all, 50 million is 50 million.

If I had started to collect jewelry, by now my entire collection, worth at least as much as my present library, could have fit in a shoebox or two.

Book Titles from Literature

I t's time for another literary game. I'm going to give you a title of a book and you tell me whether the title was taken from literature. For example, if I say the book is titled, FOR WHOM THE BELL TOLLS by Ernest Hemingway, you say it was taken from a John Donne poem or holy sonnet written in 1624. And if you say it was "Meditation XVII [17]", you get extra credit. And if you are a real smartie, you can correct the original, by telling me John Donne wrote:

"PERCHANCE he for whom this bell tolls may be so ill,as that he knows not it tolls for him."

Ready? Here's the first one: NO MAN IS AN ISLAND. That is a direct quote from... John Donne, "Meditation XVII" again. The entire quotation is:

"No man is an island, entire of itself;
every man is a piece of the continent,
a part of the main."

As far as I know, no book had that title until 1955, when the Trappist monk, Thomas Merton used it for the title of his book of essays or meditations on the spiritual life.

Lest you think this whole game will be about John Donne's works, here's something completely different. The book title is THE ROAD LESS TRAVELED by M. Scott Peck. And the original phrase was from... Robert Frost's poem. Extra credit: the poem was titled, "The Road Not Taken." And here is the entire phrase from that poem:

"Two roads diverged in a wood, and I —
I took the one less traveled by,
and that has made all the difference."

Are you getting the hang of this game? Here's another one. The book title is FROM HERE TO ETERNITY by James Jones. The phrase was from... "Gentlemen-Rankers," an 1892 poem by Rudyard Kipling about enlisted men who became commissioned officers because of their background, education, and social standing. The entire phrase from that poem:

> "We're poor little lambs who've lost our way,
> Baa! Baa! Baa!
> We're little black sheep who've gone astray,
> Baa—aa—aa!
> Gentlemen-rankers out on the spree,
> Damned from here to Eternity."

Here's another book title: THE GRAPES OF WRATH by John Steinbeck. The phrase was from the 1861 poem... "The Battle Hymn of the Republic," by Julia Ward Howe. The entire phrase from that poem:

> "Mine eyes have seen the glory of the coming of the Lord:
> He is trampling out the vintage where the grapes of wrath are stored;
> He hath loosed the fatal lightning of his terrible swift sword:
> His truth is marching on."

And another book title: I SING THE BODY ELECTRIC, the 1969 short story collection by Ray Bradbury that includes the story of the same title. The phrase was from the 1861 collection of poems... LEAVES OF GRASS, by Walt Whitman. The entire phrase from one of the 1855 poems, "I Sing the Body Electric":

31

I SING the Body electric;
The armies of those I love engirth me, and
I engirth them;
They will not let me off till I go with
them, respond to them,
And discorrupt them, and charge them full
with the charge
Of the Soul.

Here's the last title for now: the 1952 book, EAST OF EDEN, another one by John Steinbeck. The phrase was from... the Bible, Genesis 4:16. The entire phrase from that verse:

"And Cain went out from the presence of
the LORD,
and dwelt in the land of Nod, on the
east of Eden."

If you locate the source of Tom Wolfe's 1965 book of essays, THE KANDY-KOLORED TANGERINE-FLAKE STREAMLINE BABY, please let me know. It must be out there somewhere.

Building My Insult Vocabulary

For the language with the most words, English can be disappointing. Take the number of insults I might want to use at a typical cocktail party. The words are woefully inadequate, especially after libations have loosened my inhibitions.

But I recently discovered a few words that might help me put other people down. If the people who hear these insults can understand them, they are sure to be taken aback, if not downright insulted.

For example, the word *cockalorum* sounds sort of pastoral to me, like a sunny landscape filled with bright yellow flowers of the same name. But it's definitely not pastoral. It refers to a boastful and self-important person -- a strutting little fellow.

Unfortunately, just about all of the boastful people I know are not little. They're big and boisterous. So, as much as I might like to, I don't have much chance of calling them cockalorums.

Now some cockalorums are also mumpsimuses, stubborn people who insist on making an error in spite of being told they are wrong. I suppose a fellow can make errors like a mumpsimus without being a cockalorum. That would happen if he were not as small as the average strutting little cockalorum.

Many of us learned in high school that obsequious means servilely compliant. A person who is obsequious is sometimes called a bootlicker. But that isn't the word I want to rely on. The almost-unknown word I can utilize is

33

lickspittle, a fawning subordinate, like the character Dwight in the TV show, "The Office." We've all seen them in the corporate world, and now I've identified a name for them: lickspittles. I'll wager it's a word that I'll find hard to suppress at least a few times a day.

A lickspittle is not to be confused with a *milksop*, who is an unmanly man. But then again, can you be a manly man and a lickspittle at the same time? That would be quite a trick, maybe even the subject of a future -- and I might say hilarious -- sitcom.

Almost the opposite of a lickspittle is a *smellfungus*, one who finds many faults in other people. Some people are married to smellfunguses (or should I say smellfungi?) and I feel sorry for them. My father used to say, "it's easy to criticize," but he would have used a more colorful apothem if he had known about the smellfungus.

Lawyers often have a reputation of being unprincipled and shrewd, but did you know you can shorten this definition by calling them -- or anyone else, actually -- a *snollygoster?* The next time you feel cheated by a distrustful person, feel free to call him a snollygoster. He may even take it as a compliment. This word, snollygoster, has quite a bit in common with pettifogger, usually reserved for underhanded or disreputable lawyers.

Sorry to give you too many choices when you want to insult a lawyer, like the lawyer on the other side of your controversy, but I can solve the problem easily by calling him or her a snollygostering pettifogger. If I practice a little bit, I'm sure the phrase will just roll off my tongue.

Playing the game of opposites again, if the person is not a snollygoster, maybe he's a *ninnyhammer*, one who is a simpleton or a fool. Maybe the word *ninny* is short for ninnyhammer. It's hard to believe that the two words were derived independently, but I'm no etymologist, Jim, as Star Trek's Dr. McCoy might have declared.

A *mooncalf* is also a simpleton, but more of a forgetful or absentminded simpleton. As my Hungarian mother mutters under her breath sometimes, "*Sagan.*" That means "poor thing". It's not really an insult, but merely a condescending observation.

It seems unfair to pick on a young man for being awkward or gawky, but if I give in to that irresistible impulse, I might call him a *hobbledehoy* without offending him.

To summarize, even if I were a strutting cockalorum or an obstinate mumpsimus, anxious to discover faults like a smellfungus, it would be a faux pas to call a lickspittle or a milksop a word like ninnyhammer or mooncalf unless, of course, I'm more of a snollygoster than I like to think I am.

Dictionary of Obscure Sorrows

*T*he *Dictionary of Obscure Sorrows* is a compendium of invented words written by John Koenig, who is a graphic designer and film maker. He started a blog project and it's exploded into a multi-page, online dictionary that assigns words to sad emotions people feel, but don't have a word for, until now. John Koenig also narrates short descriptive videos he's created about these words. They are on YouTube.

I started browsing the dictionary on the Internet, one word after another, watching related YouTube videos, but I never got to the end. One reason I didn't finish was because John Koenig has created an immense database. The other reason is that, as I learned the definitions of the words, I became overwhelmingly depressed.

It's impressive how many obscure emotions John Koenig identified and, just as impressive, how many words he's invented for them. Here are a few words to give you an idea of the sorts of obscure emotions John Koenig has identified.

Monachopsis: The subtle but persistent feeling of being out of place. This feeling can happen at parties, weddings, and during IRS audits. I speak from experience.

Vellichor: The strange wistfulness of used bookshops somehow infused with the passage of time and filled with thousands of old books you'll never have time to read. I feel that way when I enter certain rooms in my house.

Rubatosis: The unsettling awareness of your own heartbeat. I have rubatosis and heavy breathing due to exertion at the same time. In fact, every time I ascend the stairs in my house in the Rocky Mountains, I'm experiencing rubatosis. Now, just thinking about such exertion is causing me to perspire. I wonder if there's a word for that.

Mauerbauertraurigkeit: The inexplicable urge to push people away, even close friends who you really like. This inexplicable urge is opposed to the same urge that occurs due to onions or garlic you ate for lunch. We need a word for that urge, John.

Jouska: A hypothetical conversation that you compulsively play out in your head. This happens to me after I've had an unsatisfactory exchange with a co-worker, a bully, or my wife.

Chrysalism: The amniotic tranquility of being indoors during a thunderstorm. Chrysalism isn't actually a sad emotion, but it's an emotion that needed an identifying word. So thank you, John.

Vemodalen: The frustration of photographing something amazing when thousands of identical photos already exist. It's an even stronger emotion for me when I realize that I, myself have photographed it before. What's the word for that, John?

Ellipsism: A sadness that you'll never be able to know how history will turn out. I've experienced ellipsis for many years, just dying to know what the world will be like 500 years from now and wondering if flight attendants will still be instructing travelers how to fasten their seatbelts.

Exulansis: The tendency to give up trying to talk about an experience because people are unable to relate to it. For me, this occurs most frequently when I discuss virtually any topic with my daughters.

Adronitis: Frustration with how long it takes to get to know someone. For instance, I've been trying to get to know

37

Kim Basinger since 1992 when she appeared in the movie *Cool World*.

Nodus Tollens: The realization that the plot of your life doesn't make sense to you anymore. I haven't reached that point yet, but I probably should have about 30 years ago.

Liberosis: The desire to care less about things. I've already achieved liberosis when it comes to knowing the names of young singers whose records are played on A.M. radio.

Occhiolism: The awareness of the smallness of your perspective. We all have that feeling when we look up at a star-filled sky, don't we? Talk about depressing.

So next time you find yourself having too much fun and you want to tone down your happiness a few notches, check out John Koenig's online *Dictionary of Obscure Sorrows* or his YouTube videos. You'll find an emotion that you can relate to. And you won't have to make up a word for it.

Don't Do This

We all know and some of us follow, more or less, the Ten Commandments. But did you know the Old Testament actually includes 613 commandments? Some are positive and, of course, more are negative. Specifically 248 are positive commandments, things like love God, fear God, rest on the seventh day, and burn a city that has turned to idol worship.

More interesting, though, are the 365 prohibitions. The Bible warns us not to practice astrology, magic, sorcery, or witchcraft. In fact, the Bible says we should not suffer anyone practicing witchcraft to live.

We are not supposed to attempt to contact the dead. Don't remove the signs of leprosy, the Bible tells us. As a more practical matter these days, we should not tattoo ourselves. A man shouldn't wear a woman's holy garments or vice versa, even if it's only on a music video. And never wear garments made of wool and linen mixed together. Don't ask me why. Just follow the rule and no one gets hurt.

Here's another caution to avoid injury: kidnapping your brother is forbidden. So is selling him as a slave to strangers.

We are not permitted to curse parents or teachers or the deaf, even if we do it in a soft voice.

Some of the rules would be difficult for us to obey now, like do not abhor an Edomite who repents. If I ever should encounter an Edomite, I guess I'll have to confirm that he has repented before deciding not to hate him. Anyway, that seems to conflict with the prohibition against hating anyone. Life isn't always simple, even with the Bible to guide us.

If you hang someone, don't allow his body to remain overnight. I guess that could freak out your neighbors.

Do not remove the poles from the Ark of the Covenant if you ever stumble upon it like Indiana Jones.

Don't use dishonest weights and measures. In fact, merely possessing inaccurate weights and measures is prohibited.

Do not eat the Passover lamb raw or boiled. Barbecued is still okay, I think. And whatever you do, don't let a hired servant eat some of the Passover lamb. In fact, if a person has not been circumcised, he's out of luck, too.

We can eat some types of meat, of course, but it's got to be cooked well done, until it is white inside with no tinge of red or pink. So if you're a medium rare person, you've been sinning all along. Drunkenness is prohibited. It turns out, even after drinking one too many cocktails, you have no excuse for ordering your steak rare. And for the love of God, never eat the meat of a bull that has been stoned to death for goring someone.

The Bible has a lot to say about animal sacrifices and offerings. I'm going to skip that topic for now, since I'm still trying to digest the well-done meat advice.

Speaking of food, we are not permitted to eat worms found in fruit or produce. In other words, if you bite into an apple and you see half a worm where you just bit, it's best to spit out the other half. If you don't, indigestion may not be the worst of your problems.

Oh, and we are not to destroy fruit trees. Ever. Simple enough, but what if one of them is growing in the middle of an airport runway?

If you're a Nazirite, you've got a whole bunch or should I say "bunches," of things you can't eat or drink: fresh grapes or any beverage made from grapes; raisins; grape seeds; or grape skins. In other words, there's something about grapes and Nazirites that just isn't kosher.

As a farmer, you have to be careful not to gather all the olives from your trees or all the grapes from your vineyard, since the remaining fruits are for the poor. Also, don't plant a field or a vineyard with two kinds of seed.

A rancher is prohibited from crossbreeding different species of animals, even if they consent, the way I read it. In fact, a farmer or rancher can't even work with two different species of animals yoked together.

Sex is a touchy subject in the Bible. You cannot have sexual relations with your mother, your father's wife, your sister, your half-sister, your daughter, or your granddaughter. Also forbidden is having sex with your father's sister, your mother's sister, or your father's brother's wife.

When it comes to marriage, be sure you don't marry both a woman and her daughter, or both a woman and her granddaughter. If you're a priest, I'm afraid you can't marry a harlot. Moreover, a High Priest can't marry a divorced woman or a widow, regardless of whether she's also a harlot.

And, as if you have any control over this, don't allow your daughter to play the harlot or fornicate.

Finally, a man must not allow himself to be castrated. I'm not a biblical scholar, but that sounds like good advice to me.

First Printing of a Word

I'm always surprised at how long certain words have been used before I learn about them.

For example, did you know the word *humongous* was in print more than 50 years ago in 1967? Or that *quark* and *condo* and *soul food* and *garage sale* and *zip-code* and *golden years* and *training wheels* were all introduced the same year, 1964?

Exactly 300 years before that, in 1664, *mug, greenhouse, sleeping pill, colossal, gimp, Irish potato, shallot,* and *celery* made their first appearance in print. I wonder what they used to call celery before that.

In a minute, I'm going to give you the website that's been indispensable to me to learn about the first use of these words. But I wanted to tell you that the website will let you see all of the words that were introduced in a given year and you can search any specific word to find out when it was first printed.

Here's a test to show you how much fun that website can be. What word came before the expression, *diving bell* in 1661? Was it *flatulency, milestone,* or *vanilla*? The answer is *flatulency* in 1660. *Milestone* and *vanilla* appeared a year after *diving bell*, in 1662. Now don't tell me I didn't prepare you for a fun discussion at your next cocktail party.

How do I know this extreme trivia, the stuff that even the TV show, *Jeopardy*, wouldn't touch? The answer is the online version of the Merriam-Webster dictionary, www.merrriam-webster.com/time-traveler. Next time you have an hour or two, check that website out. Oh, *website.* First appeared in print in 1993.

Full of It

What do the words *hopeful*, *joyful*, *healthful*, *helpful*, *colorful*, and *doubtful* have in common? They all express definite, extreme conditions. Hopeful means full of hope, doubtful means full of doubt, etc. They're all useful words. Hey, useful; that's another one.

But there are times the glass is not entirely full, when the emotion we're expressing is merely beyond a reasonable doubt, not 100%. I think it's time to add a few more adjectives to the list of emotions.

What if you're not absolutely, 100% full of some emotion, but only pretty full. Maybe it's just wishful thinking – oops, there I go again – but I think equivocating words can be used occasionally. For example, if something scared me, like being audited by the IRS, but I wasn't debilitated with fear, I'd like to say I wasn't full of fear, but merely fear-ish or perhaps dread-ish or fret-ish or fright-ish or even stress-ish.

Similarly, I might think a woman is fairly young, but not full of youth, so I could say she's youth-ish. Maybe youth-ish and beauty-ish and cheer-ish and play-ish. And I'd assume she was faith-ish, if that were the case. Certainly not harm-ish or hurt-ish or sin-ish, although I wouldn't mind a bit lust-ish.

So let's give it a try. Start using "ish" instead of "full" when the occasion arises and you don't want to come across too pompously. Don't be bash-ish or the other extreme, boast-ish. Instead, be thought-ish and tact-ish and somewhat glee-ish. My suggestion isn't pain-ish, but fruit-ish and I am thank-ish for your attention.

International Idioms

Idioms are expressions that can't be understood from the meanings of their separate words, but have separate meanings of their own. For example, the phrase *we're on the same page* has nothing to do with pages or books, but merely indicates we both agree with each other or we think the same way. Believe me, this is an authentic definition of idioms. I wouldn't pull your leg because I don't want you thinking this is the last straw.

I started to wonder whether our American idioms translate well into other languages. One thing led to another, as they often do when I'm browsing the Internet, and I found a website with foreign idioms that I hadn't heard before.

Needless to say, I couldn't wait to share them with you, my long-suffering audience. For a change, I'll spare you my clumsy attempts at pronouncing the phrases in their original languages. I'll use an approximate English translation, instead.

A few idioms in foreign languages refer to what we Americans mean when we say *when pigs fly* to mean it's never going to happen. For example, the expression in Spanish is *when frogs grow hair*. And in Thailand they say *when the 7-11 is closed*. In Thailand, to express the thought that it's not going to happen, they say *one afternoon in your next reincarnation*. The French express this sentiment as *when chicken have teeth*. I've noticed that many idioms, especially French idioms, include food items, as you would expect.

In America, we say *the early bird gets the worm,* meaning success comes to those who prepare well and put in effort. I always thought it was a Ben Franklin proverb, but the phrase was actually first recorded 36 years before Gentle Ben was born, in John Ray's collection of English proverbs 1670. It turns out that the same proverb is expressed by Italians as *he who sleeps doesn't catch any fish.* Swedes say *first to the mill gets to grind first.* And Germans say *morning has gold in its mouth.*

When a German means don't beat around the bush, he says, *don't talk around the hot porridge.* When he wants to ask for special treatment, he asks for an extra sausage.

When a German says *you have tomatoes on your eyes,* he means you are oblivious about what is going around you. The Germans use food items in their idioms, too.

When Germans want to acknowledge that it will be a good party, they will say *the bear dances there.*

Clear as dumpling broth means crystal clear. To have a pig means to have a stroke of luck. When a German wants to put his two cents in, he *adds his mustard.*

Speaking of mustard, when the French mean I'm getting angry, they say *the mustard is getting to my nose.*

When a French person wants to say somebody is completely useless, she says *that person doesn't know how to do anything with his ten fingers.*

To *arrive like the hair in a soup* refers to entering a situation at the most awkward moment possible. We've all been there, like a hair in a soup.

To have a *fat morning* means to sleep in. And *a strike of lightning* refers to love at first sight. I think I can use both of those, but I'll have to work on my French pronunciation.

To *put a rabbit on somebody* means to stand somebody up.

When a French person believes a situation can't be changed, he will say *the carrots are cooked.*

Latvians may want someone to go away or leave them alone. They say *go pick mushrooms!*

The Russians say *there's no truth in your legs*, which means sit down.

And for a Russian, *don't push the horses* means don't be in a rush.

To think someone is stubborn, a Russian will say *you can sharpen an ax on top of his head.* That's probably easier to do if the stubborn guy happens to be German and has tomatoes on his eyes.

I'm not a horseradish from a mountain to a Russian means, of course, I'm a special person.

Bet you can't guess what *I have a lot of grandmothers* means. The Russian idiom means *I'm very rich* or *I have a lot of money.*

In Thailand, when they say *eat like a pig, live like a dog*, they mean you're messy and untidy.

And in Thailand, being a spendthrift is referred to as *a bamboo basket with a leaky bottom.*

The Thai expression for investing a lot for a little return is *ride an elephant to catch grasshoppers.*

When two people know each other's secrets, they say *the hen sees the snake's feet and the snake sees the hen's boobs.*

And here's a word of caution for Thai adventurers: *enter the forest, but don't forget to take your machete.* That means *be cautious.* That's good advice for all of us, even if we're not planning to enter a forest.

A modest Japanese person may refer to a small piece of land he owns as *big as a cat's forehead.*

Croatians say *a pussycat will come to the tiny door*, when they mean *what comes around goes around*.

Koreans who want to express the American idiom *six of one, half a dozen of the other* say *fifty steps are similar to one hundred steps*. They must be on the metric system, I'm thinking.

The Dutch admire a person who buys an object for a low price. They say *he bought it for an apple and an egg*.

We know the American idiom *he's made a mountain out of a molehill*, but the Swedes say *he's made a hen out of a feather*.

We may caution *don't bite off more than you can chew*, but the Swedes say *don't take water over your head*. They also caution people not to worry by saying *there's no cow on the ice* or *there's no danger on the roof*.

Sometimes Swedes will resent a person who didn't have to work to get where he is. The expression they use is *he slid in on a shrimp sandwich*. We might say that person was born with a silver spoon in his mouth. Now doesn't that make a way more lot of sense?

A Portuguese person does not cause problems – he *breaks all the dishes*.

For the Portuguese, you are not just sexy, you are *good as corn*.

On the other hand, if you're not as good as corn, you should make the most of what you've got. The Portuguese will say *if you don't have a dog, hunt with a cat*.

They don't just shut up and listen to things they don't like. They *swallow frogs*. And if they keep postponing a chore, they're known to *push something with their belly*.

Polish people use idioms with animals. For example, a person who cheats or misleads others *turns someone into a horse*. On the other hand, sometimes that same person may take blame for something he didn't do, in which case the Portuguese will say the fellow *had to pay the duck.*

Poles may think someone has no ear for music, so they will ask *Did an elephant stomp on your ear?*

When something drives a Pole crazy, he says *he got cat.*

When something is very easy, a Pole will say *it's a roll on butter.* We're back to food now.

So, when you visit another country, you can sound like a native. Just remember, don't push the horses, and don't take water over your head. Remember: morning has gold in its mouth. You'll be good as corn.

Middle Names

I'm going to give you plenty of advanced notice to get ready for Middle Name Pride Day this time around. Mark your calendars. My online sources list March 10th as the special day to celebrate middle names, or the first Friday of the first full week in March. But that alternative rule seems needlessly complicated. I think the middle of the month — that is, the third Wednesday of any month with five Wednesdays — would be more appropriate; but as usual, no one asked me.

A fellow named Jerry Hill got the ball rolling on middle names. He thought Middle Name Pride Day would be a good time for us to call each other by our middle names. The only people whose middle names I know are dead and it seems disrespectful to refer to the deceased by his or her middle name.

Some people are not particularly proud of their middle name; they're actually ashamed of it. President Obama, for example, suggested not giving your newborn child Hussein as a middle name if you'd like him or her to run for President someday.

Speaking of Presidents, Harry S. Truman used only his middle initial, because that's all he had. That wasn't the case for Rutherford B. Hayes or Warren G. Harding or Ulysses S. Grant, but you never hear their middle names: Birchard, Gamaliel, and Simpson, respectively. Fortunately, all of them preceded Middle Name Pride Day.

On the other hand, some folks are proud of their middle names. I'll bet you can fill in the surnames of famous

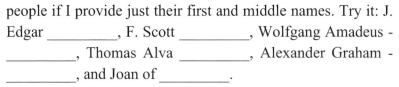

people if I provide just their first and middle names. Try it: J. Edgar _____, F. Scott _____, Wolfgang Amadeus - _____, Thomas Alva _____, Alexander Graham - _____, and Joan of _____.

Show business people don't always appear to have a last name, much less a middle one, like Cher, Madonna, Liberace, and the artist formerly known as Prince. But other celebrities would feel naked without their middle name, like Tommy Lee Jones, Jamie Lee Curtis, James Earl Jones, Billy Bob Thornton, and Francis Ford Coppola.

I can understand why certain actors keep their middle names hidden. Richard Gere's middle name is Tiffany; Tina Fey's is Stamantina; Hugh Grant's is Mungo; and Quincy Jones's, believe it or not, is Delight. And you hardly ever hear Donald Duck use his middle name: Fauntleroy.

Architect Frank Lloyd Wright wasn't ashamed or embarrassed about anything when maybe he should have been. His middle name doesn't top the list of embarrassments, especially in the eyes of his three wives and a few women married to his clients who may or may not have had middle names.

My middle name is Edward. I'm not embarrassed by it, but I never use it since it takes so long to write. When I become famous, I will hate to spend so much time signing my name for autograph hunters when I should be preparing for my appearance on The Tonight Show.

Joyce Carol Oates's name, however long, doesn't stop her from being one of the most prolific and successful authors. At last count, knocking out an average of two novels per year, she had more than 40 novels published under her name and a score of books published in a couple of her noms de plume in addition to dozens of short story collections. When I asked her to sign one of her books, she just penned her initials — yes, all three of them; but to be fair, 400 people were on line behind me, all with the same request. And she might have had a tough day when I approached her. She spends at least 10 hours every day writing long hand. Writer's cramp is a penalty for being a prolific, Luddite author.

Notorious criminals often go by their full names. In fact, nine of the twelve most heinous serial killers in the U.S. used their three names. The most famous three political assassins — Lee Harvey Oswald, James Earl Ray, and John Wilkes Booth — used three names. So did Mark David Chapman, the man who shot John Lennon.

When I was in law school, I learned about U.S. Supreme Court Chief Justices Earl Warren and then Warren Burger. It was probably a mistake on my part to discover that Warren Burger's middle name was Earl, so Earl Warren was immediately succeeded by Warren Earl... Burger. Confusing, eh? What are the odds? Even though their middle names were a source of befuddlement, the two chief justices were politically opposite so hardly anyone confuses them.

Remember Jerry Hill, the man who invented this holiday? How ironic and sad that the man who wanted to help people feel proud of their middle name didn't have one himself. It would be like Aquaman's father not knowing how to dog paddle.

My Last Words

You know how sometimes a book's title is so irresistible, the volume jumps off the shelf and into your hands? That's exactly what happened to me with an unassuming book titled *Famous Last Words* by Terry Breverton. It's a book containing hundreds of one-liners purported to be the last words of famous people uttered or proclaimed or shouted immediately before they died. What a wonderful book for morbid-minded people with short attention spans. Actually, perfect for me.

For example, Lady Astor, as we all know, was a Christian Scientist and the first woman member of Parliament in the British House of Commons. Upon awakening and being surprised by her whole family surrounding her bed, she asked, "Is it my birthday or am I dying?"

Many of us know Oscar Wilde's last quip, "either that wallpaper goes, or I do." You have to miss the fellow, even if you never met him, which is likely, seeing as how he died in 1900.

The hotel pioneer, Conrad Hilton's practical but not-so-famous last words were, "Leave the shower curtain on the inside of the tub." Now that's useful advice.

Then there are those who were in denial about their situation, right up to the end. H.G. Wells said, "Go away. I'm all right."

At his own end, the action actor Douglas Fairbanks declared, "Never felt better."

And before the early 20th century Irish novelist, Donn Byrne, got into a fatal car crash, he said, "I think I'll go for a drive before dinner. Anyone come along?" Reportedly it was a defective steering wheel that did him in.

The famous Red Baron von Richtofen, on the day he died in a dogfight, said, "Don't you think I'll come back?" There's a lesson there about being overconfident and tempting fate.

And here's another one. Union Army General John Sedgwick refused to stay behind a parapet during the Civil War, declaring, "Nonsense. They couldn't hit an elephant at this dist—."

Eighteenth century French philosopher Denis Diderot's wife chastised him about eating an apricot. He said, "What possible harm could it do to me?"

Actually, food plays a role in quite a few final words. The last words of French poet Paul Claudel, for instance, were "Do you think it could have been the sausage?"

In 2001, Todd Poller of Bixby, Missouri died by choking on a live fish but not before inviting his friends to "watch this!" It was a perch, in case you're keeping track.

Before dying of asphyxiation, Scottish footballer Alan McLaren prepared to stuff his mouth with chocolate by saying, "See how long it takes me to eat this."

On his last day, comedian Lou Costello said, "That was the best ice-cream soda I ever tasted." It was strawberry, by the way.

In 1790, the writer known as the Marquis de Favras was handed his official death sentence by radicals of the French revolution and astutely remarked, "I see you have made three spelling mistakes."

Boy, that rang a bell with me. It got me thinking that I'd like to be in a future edition of Famous Last Words. But in order to do that, I reasoned, I couldn't leave such an important, maybe immortal, phrase to chance. They might be my last words, but I shouldn't wait till the last minute to create them or rehearse them. I don't want to be remembered for something mundane, like "Please let the cat out," or "Have a nice day."

The words I leave behind should be unique, profound, and thought provoking but not too complicated. My last words should be inspirational but they shouldn't offer false hope. They should be easy for my survivors to recall and repeat. They should remain in people's minds like lyrics to a song.

As you can see, this is not a trivial matter. It's very important to me. The most memorable lyrics, the best advice, the most profound thoughts, unfortunately, have already been used. But I will not be deterred. I am working on a phrase and it is fantastic, if I must say so myself. It will set a new standard for parting words. I know you'll be impressed. But if I tell you now, it would ruin the surprise.

Out of Words

Some French translations of the Sherlock Holmes short novel, A STUDY IN SCARLET, use the word for crimson or purple, since the word "scarlet" did not exist in French in 1887. The French language has fewer than 100,000 words, and scarlet, apparently, didn't make the cut.

The German language has more words, but it's a rather terse language, as we know, not famous for many colorful adjectives and adverbs.

Spanish has no more than twice the number of French words.

Hebrew has fewer than 80,000 words, which is understandable since it has an alphabet of only 22 letters. The word *alphabet* itself is a contraction of the first two letters of the Hebrew alphabet called aleph and bet. The Old Testament was written with only 8,674 different words.

Since snow is so important to Eskimos, it's not surprising to know that the Inuit language with its suffixes can create a huge number of different words to describe snow with various characteristics from slushy to powder to frosty sparkling. I wonder how many Arabic words describe oil.

Of the 6,900 human languages and dialects, English is the language with the greatest number of words — a little over one million. William Shakespeare coined 1,700 of them.

Part of the reason English has so many words, so many synonyms, is that a good number were stolen — lexicographers like to say "borrowed" — from Latin, French, German and other languages.

Here's something that surprises me. With all the words at our disposal, why do we English speaking people have heteronyms — words that are spelled the same but pronounced differently, like a response may be inVALid but the person giving the response is an Invalid. Why do we have so many homophones — words that sound the same but differ in meaning, like moose the animal and mousse the dessert?

Lead and lead, for example, are heteronyms. Lead is the 82nd element of the periodic table but lead is a verb that means "to show the way." Things are even more complicated when you realize the lead in lead pencils is really graphite, a polymorph of carbon, element 6, for those of you who are taking notes.

Besides lead being a heteronym with lead, it is also a homophone that has a number of meanings from an advantage held by a competitor in a race, to take somebody somewhere, to the introductory section of a story, to electrical wires.

The word "thong" means an open-toed shoe or — spelled and pronounced the same way — means very skimpy beachwear or underwear. Speaking of the former, a shoe is footwear but to shoo means to push away. And tissue means Kleenex. (Just kidding, Kimberly-Clark.)

Read and read are spelled the same, even though they represent different tenses of the same verb, while the color red, spelled r-e-d, is pronounced the same as the past tense of read, just to make things more interesting.

How many words do we have to express how something smells? We can use smell and fragrance and odor and aroma and stench; but don't use scent, because that's also the name we give to the soon-to-be-obsolete monetary unit of measure. I don't know if I will be happy when the cent disappears, because the penny is such a bothersome article, or if I think it will stink, because it means nothing's left that can be bought for a penny.

I won't bore you with other examples of homophones and heteronyms, or homographs and homonyms for that matter. My point is that with all of the English words that exist and all of the combinations of letters that haven't been used, why can't we come up with new words that don't sound and aren't spelled like other words?

The color red could be something like keed, which rhymes with nosebleed, and the past tense of read could be reaked. Logical, don't you think?

The element "lead" could just as easily be called exmard, which rhymes with hard and connotes X-rays, which cannot penetrate what we used to call lead.

The shoe that I wear can be a techiggy, which connotes protection of little piggies that go to market.

I also have some great ideas about renaming that sexy bathing and underwear attire I mentioned earlier, but wouldn't you know it? I'm out of time.

Oxymorons

I was thinking about oxymorons, recently. You know, words or expressions that have internally inconsistent or opposite meanings, like black light or jumbo shrimp.

I quickly ran out of examples, yet I had a lot more time on my hands, so I turned to my ever-ready computer and found hundreds of oxymorons on a web site called adrianskiles@mindspring.com. Mr. Skiles and his buddy, John Shore, spent more time thinking about oxymorons than anyone I've ever heard of. Their list includes quite a few funny oxymorons. Some of their examples are also sarcastic, sacrilegious, or frankly, sexist. For example, they list oxymoronic expressions, which, if I were a more sensitive sort of guy, could offend me. Here they are:

> Faithful boyfriend
> Man's intuition
> Male compassion, and even
> Adult male.

Granted, these are difficult to argue with. One wonders, though, if Adrian and John got help from women.

I really took umbrage at their examples of oxymorons that were "clearly ambiguous," aiming at my esteemed profession. But there was no way I could turn a "blind eye" to them. Here they are:

> Decent lawyer
> Ethical attorney

Honest lawyer, and
Reasonable attorney fees.

I hardly see the humor in those, do you?

Mr. Skiles and company didn't limit themselves to people, though. They also shared their views on music with a list of what they deem to be oxymorons:

Accordion music
Country music
Rap music, and
Disco music.

And when they were finished with that form of popular culture, they shifted to the gastronomic. Here are their food oxymorons:

Unsalted saltines
White chocolate
Diet ice cream
Fried ice cream, and
12-ounce pound cake.

They also believed that cafeteria food, school food, and, of course, airline food are all oxymorons.

Finally, they pointed out that the names of certain foods are inherently suspect, like:

Sweet tarts
Cotton candy
Boneless ribs, and
Hard water.

As you can see, some of the oxymorons on their list are "awfully good." I couldn't think of even one that was "found missing." As you know, it's "old news" that I don't have time to give you more than a "detailed summary," although I'd give "even odds" on starting a "new tradition" in the "immediate future," even at the risk of presenting a "press release" of an expanded session that goes over like a "lead balloon" when I'm trying to "act naturally." But that may be my "only choice."

Hey, it wouldn't be the first time that my listeners' reaction was "cold as hell." That's the reason I wear my "tight slacks."

If you haven't had enough of these morsels, do check out adrianskiles@mindspring.com.

Shakespeare's Words

Quick, who invented skim milk? How about luggage? And the whirligig? What about the buzzer? Well, I don't know who invented any of them, but I do know who used their names first in the English language: William Shakespeare.

You may have heard of William Shakespeare. If you've gotten beyond 7th grade, for better or worse you were probably exposed to at least one of his literary works. In addition to his 37 plays, Shakespeare contributed some 1,100 words and phrases to the English language — everything from "set my teeth on edge" to "wild goose chase" to "what the dickens" to "faint hearted" to "in my heart of hearts" to "sick at heart" to "wear my heart upon my sleeve," as opposed to "heart of gold," also Shakespeare.

And speaking of gold, remember it was Shakespeare who said, "all that glitters is not gold."

You'll have to imagine me making "air quotes" as I tell you Shakespeare was the first to "break the ice" by "playing fast and loose" with the "naked truth," even at the risk of being a "laughing stock" and affecting his "spotless reputation" all the "live long day." It's "cold comfort" that the poor guy has "seen better days" but now has "breathed his last" and is "dead as a doornail." A "sorry sight," indeed. But I would certainly not say "good riddance" to the fellow who observed, "love is blind."

Most of these phrases are now really household words. As a matter of fact, he even coined "household words."

When it comes to short phrases, certain book titles come right out of Shakespeare. There's:

"Something Wicked This Way Comes,"
"Sound and Fury," and
"Brave New World."

The one who first said, "the better part of valor is discretion" wasn't the Cowardly Lion; it was Shakespeare. And the fellow who "refused to budge an inch" wasn't originally General Patton; it was Shakespeare. The person who complained that someone had "eaten me out of house and home" wasn't Archie Bunker; it was Shakespeare.

"The game is afoot," wasn't first said by Sherlock Holmes; it was Shakespeare.

And who do you think first said, "A diamond as big as the Ritz?" No, it was F. Scott Fitzgerald, I think. That was a trick question to see if you were listening.

But back to Shakespeare. He invented a few verbs you may recognize. Here are just some of them, in alphabetical order:

to arouse
to bump
to cater
to drug
to educate, and
to elbow

He also used "elbow room" first; guess Billy, as his friends probably called him, had a thing for elbow, along with hearts.

There are even more verbs invented by Shakespeare:

65

to outgrow
to petition
to supervise, and
to undress.

Your children may drive you crazy with a Sherlockian phrase, because it was the immortal bard who first asked the immortal question, "Knock, knock. Who's there?" For the answer to that one, you'll have to see Macbeth.

I could go on, but I think I've come "full circle" and, as someone once said, "brevity is the soul of wit."

Simplifying English

My maternal grandmother was born in Hungary in 1901 and emigrated to the U.S. early enough for her to attend public schools here, from grade school through high school. She received as good an education as the city of New York could provide a pretty, young girl who valued beauty over academics.

She's no longer with us, but some of her dialect lingers in my memory. One of her habits was to pronounce English words just as they are spelled. Maybe that helped her remember how to spell them or maybe she just wanted to lord her pronunciations over her schoolmates.

I recall her soft, kindly voice pronouncing every syllable like this: "Come visit me in Feb-ru-ar-y, dear Markie, and we'll have an int-er-est-ing time. First we'll go to the li-bra-ry and then I'll make car-a-mel apples and veg-et-a-ble soup to warm you up and make you com-fort-a-ble in my con-do-min-i-um even if the temp-er-a-ture outside is chilly."

I don't often hear people speak like that unless English is their second language. Abbreviating and slurring are more frequent. As our spoken language has evolved over the centuries, of course, pronunciations and then spellings have changed.

Some people have tried to update spelling rules in advance of the natural evolution of language, but with little success. For example, George Bernard Shaw and Andy Rooney attempted to reform English linguistics by eliminating the apostrophe to indicate an elision in written documents. Shaw thought they were mostly redundant. Sometimes the meaning of the word might be confused with other words. For instance, the contraction of "she will" without an apostrophe would be pronounced "shell," so they spelled that word with an apostrophe, the way we are used to seeing it.

I just know it wasn't Shaw's idea to add a "p" to psychology, psychiatrist, psychotic, and psychoanalysis. Aren't those words long enough as they are? That "p" addition was just plain psycho and the rule can drive me crazy. Speaking of medical conditions, don't get me started on the adjective, "phthisic," which we all know describes people with the lung disease, "phthisis." All the "h's" in that word are silent, and so is the "p."

Many words are almost always mispronounced, so I agree with Shaw to some extent: we should change their spelling to catch up to the audible expressions. Try these on for size: expresso, vetinarian, Isreal, pecahn with an "h," gahla with an "h," vahz with an "h," and fwah grah with a couple of "h's."

I'd like to change Worcestershire — both the British city and the steak sauce — to Werstersure.

And while I'm at it, after I read a book, I've read it. Can't we spell *read* and *read* as differently as we pronounce them? We already do that for feed and fed.

Since I haven't spoken Latin since my bar mitzvah, the "b" in debt makes no sense to me. Does it to you?

I would drop the "a" in temperament and no one would miss it. I'll bet a lot of people don't know it's supposed to be there anyway. Only my grandmother ever pronounced it. Ditto for the mountain range, Himalayas. Aren't three "a's" a bit of overkill?

68

And I would add a "d" to the "g" in pigeon; at least until those birds start to take umbrage at that wordage.

Taking Things to a Whole New, Very Unique Level, and Other Overused Expressions

A re you tired of broadcast advertisers telling you their products represent a whole new level of performance or convenience or glamour? I never hear real people in regular, private conversation talking about whole new levels of anything.

And what's that "whole" about anyway? Can something represent a fractional new level? How do you measure a whole level of convenience? With a ruler or a bathroom weighing scale or what?

How do you know whether you've achieved a whole new level of convenience or merely a bit more convenience on the same level? Advertisers never say they have more of the same old level of convenience. That would make more sense than claiming a whole new level has been achieved, but that doesn't pack the same punch. A whole new level definitely impresses me, even if I don't know what they're talking about.

Sometimes television promos state that I can watch a whole new episode of my favorite series tomorrow. Actually, I've never seen an episode that wasn't a whole new one. It's either an old episode that I've seen already or a new one; but it's never an episode that's only partly new. So why tell me it's a whole new episode?

You've undoubtedly heard the expression, "slippery slope," as in "once you legalize marijuana, you're on a slippery slope to harder drugs." Now that I'm in Colorado, I've experienced many more slippery slopes than I ever did in Florida, but if a slippery slope existed for every time I've heard the expression, our whole planet would be unnavigable. I'd be careening into other people and things every time I left my home, even if I don't ever sample the killer weed.

Similarly, there aren't enough icebergs in the north Atlantic to support all the times I've heard the "tip of the iceberg" phrase. The expression means a bigger problem or controversy exists than we know. I guess the expression is nice shorthand for the concept that things will inevitably get worse. That would help explain why I can't help re-living scenes from the Titanic movie every time I hear the music, especially when I'm on a boat.

Just as broadcast advertisers are the only ones who throw around whole new levels, we normal people are the only ones who modify the word "unique" with adjectives. Broadcasters don't do that. Only regular folks abuse the word "unique." They don't merely say something is unique. They have to say it's "sort of unique" or "pretty unique" or "very unique."

Now the word "unique" is defined as "the only one of its kind." So, saying something is very unique is like saying someone is very pregnant. Either you are or you aren't. Either something is or isn't the only one of its kind. It doesn't make sense to say something is extremely one of its kind, does it? When you say something is unique, that's the end of it. You can't get any higher than the top of the mountain. No need to add an adjective.

The next time I hear someone say something is very unique, I'm going to tell him his usage is the tip of the iceberg of his reliance on inappropriate expressions and he's on a slippery slope towards illiteracy. If you ask me, he ought to try for a whole new level of grammar.

The S Word and the F Word

We live in an enlightened era and culture; I think you'll agree. Unless our actions are likely to harm others, we can get away with a lot of activities that would have been shocking to our grandparents, much less to our great-grandparents. For example, nowadays, we go to the beach and wear bathing suits that don't extend from our neck to our toes. We travel on airplanes in jeans and sneakers — a far cry from the suits and dresses that our grandparents used to wear. More cowboys wear baseball hats than the sort of cowboy hats that Gene Autry used to wear. The other day, believe it or not, I even saw someone chew gum in public.

That's why it's hard to understand why the food industry has become so sensitive, even puritanical. Have you noticed that the S word has basically been removed from food packages?

Breakfast cereal has taken the biggest hit. What used to be Sugar Smacks is now sold in our grocery stores as Honey Crisp or, for even more sensitive consumers, Golden Crisp.

Sugar Frosted Flakes are now simply Frosted Flakes. Sugar Pops are now Corn Pops. Sugar coated shredded wheat is now frosted mini wheats. Yes, the sugar content of some of these products still takes up more than 50% of their weight, and it's a fact: there is more sugar in a serving of Golden Crisp than in a glazed donut. But all the more reason to proclaim and embrace, not suppress the word, sugar, on the boxes. Whatever happened to truth in advertising? I guess cereal companies think that when they change the name, we believe sugar, the number one ingredient, magically disappears.

So, we'll be seeing fewer and fewer products that include the S word — sugar — in their trademark in the future.

YIKES! The days left for sugar beets and sugar snap peas may be numbered, too. Come to think of it, doesn't the Southeast Football Conference still play in the Sugar Bowl in New Orleans, or has it been renamed the Golden Crisp Bowl?

On the other hand, farmers and woodsmen stubbornly hold on to their sugarhouses for boiling tree sap into maple syrup every year. And, of course, young starlets will always need their sugar daddies, which is good news for them, I suppose.

The S word isn't the only one that may disappear. The F word is endangered, too. Lately, I've been noticing fewer "chicken fried steaks" on restaurant menus, replaced with "smothered steak" or "country style steak."

In fact, a whole restaurant chain has been transformed. Col. Sanders' beloved Kentucky Fried Chicken is now known only by its initials, KFC. I can see the colonel now, spinning in his grave like a chicken leg in its batter. Surprisingly, the dreaded F still appears in KFC, even now, when KFC is advertising grilled or "unfried" chicken more often — in the northern states, at least — than its fried, and tastier counterpart.

From their recent TV commercials, KFC doesn't even appear to sell fried chicken anymore, which is too bad, because I really like that more than any other food... except maybe deep-fried sugar plums.

What Shakespeare Never Said

Did you know Sherlock Holmes never said, "Elementary, my dear Watson?" He said "elementary" only eight times in the 60 Arthur Conan Doyle stories, but never exactly "Elementary, my dear Watson." And while I'm on the subject, "The game is afoot," wasn't first said by Sherlock Holmes; it was Shakespeare.

We tend to remember quotations and their narrators the way we want to, or the way others have fed them to us. Frankly, some of the ways we remember the quotations are better than the originals, but that's not the point. (This is where you probably expect me to tell what the point of this essay is, but I'm as clueless as you.) Let me give you a few more examples of Shakespearean quotations that almost everyone remembers incorrectly.

"Methinks the lady doth protest too much" is close to Shakespeare's original in Hamlet, but no cigar. Queen Gertrude actually said "The lady doth protest too much, methinks."

And speaking of cigars, the comment attributed to Sigmund Freud, "Sometimes a cigar is just a cigar" originally started out as "Sometimes a pipe is just a pipe." But that doesn't pack the wallop of the better-known misquotation. You have to admit, though, either one is better than "Sometimes a cigarette is just a cigarette."

Now back to the Bard. William Shakespeare didn't write "All that glistens is not gold" or "All that glitters is not gold." What he said in The Merchant of Venice was "All that glisters is not gold." We don't use "glisters" much anymore.

It's certainly not as popular a word as "luggage." Shakespeare coined the word, "luggage," but you can't blame him for when the airlines lose it.

How about "Lead on, Macduff?" Shakespeare in Macbeth, right? Nope, he wrote "Lay on, Macduff, and damned be him who first cries 'Hold! Enough!'" I don't know anyone who quotes that one accurately.

"Bubble bubble, toil and trouble" is another Shakespearean misquotation. It was actually "Double, double toil and trouble" in Macbeth. Bubbles weren't as plentiful in the 17th century as they are now, since our national drink became Coca-Cola.

In Romeo and Juliet, William Shakespeare didn't write "A rose by any other name smells just as sweet." He wrote "What's in a name? That which we call a rose by any other word would smell as sweet." True, the original is longer, but more poetic, methinks.

That's enough Shakespeare for now, methinks again. Let's discuss other classics.

In The Wizard of Oz, remember Dorothy saying "Toto, I don't think we're in Kansas anymore?" In fact, she said, "Toto, I've a feeling we're not in Kansas anymore." Big difference, especially for those of us who care what Dorothy feels when she's not belting out, "Somewhere Over the Rainbow." By the way, the original title to that song was "Who Knows What's Over the Rainbow." Just kidding. Sorry, Ms. Garland.

In The Silence of the Lambs, Hannibal Lecter doesn't say, "Hello, Clarice" in that creepy voice. He says, "Good evening, Clarice." Same creepy voice, but substituting two words for "hello" makes it more formal and even more creepy.

The famous line in Field of Dreams isn't "If you build it, they will come." It's "If you build it, he will come." That definitely doesn't sound as good as the version we all remember, but it's too late to reshoot the movie.

One of the most famous misquotations is in Snow White and the Seven Dwarfs. The queen doesn't ask "Mirror mirror on the wall, who is the fairest one of all?" She actually says, "Magic mirror on the wall, who is the fairest one of all?" Either way, of course, the queen was not amused with the answer.

And speaking of queens, it's hard to believe, but there is no record of Queen Victoria ever saying, "we are not amused." Now that's a bit of trivia that I find, um, interesting.

Remember the TV series, Dragnet? In the original, Jack Webb as Sgt. Joe Friday never said "Just the facts, ma'am," even though we can see him say that in our mind's eye as clearly as that old black and white DuMont TV set in our parents' living room.

W.C. Fields didn't suggest "I would rather be in Philadelphia" for his tombstone, but "I would rather be living in Philadelphia." What he meant was "I'd rather be living, even in Philadelphia, than dead anywhere else." I suppose, when you're dead you'd rather be living. People always want what they can't have.

Remember Tennyson's line from The Charge of the Light Brigade, "Theirs is but to do or die?" Wrong. It was actually "Theirs not to reason why, Theirs but to do and die." That's less of a choice and more of a reproductive drone ant's prime directive.

Speaking of prime directives, Star Trek's original Captain Kirk of the USS Enterprise never said, "Beam me up, Scotty." He said "Beam me aboard" and "Beam us up home" and "Two to beam up." Alas, poor Scotty!, as Shakespeare might have said. I knew him, Horatio.

Dr. McCoy on the same TV series never said "damn it," as in "Damn it, Jim! I'm a doctor, not an intellectual property attorney." You see, Dr. McCoy never cursed.

Oliver Twist didn't say "Please, Sir, can I have some more?" He was more demanding, actually saying "Please, Sir, I want some more."

Finally, Shakespeare didn't write "To gild the lily." He wrote "To gild refined gold, to paint the lily." Now, painting lilies sounds delicate and beautiful to me. But damn it, I'm an essayist, not a horticulturalist.

What the Bible Left Out

The Bible is indispensable for many of us. Not only is it a source of comfort, but it's a comprehensive guide for people to live meaningful, ethical lives. And, of course, it's the basis for the last word in many a quarrel. It's hard to argue with a man who cites scripture to bolster his elevated moral positions.

It is estimated that the Bible has been printed about six billion times, making it the best-selling book of all time, even surpassing Quotations from Chairman Mao, which was distributed to a mere 900 million people.

The Bible is a source of prophecies and predictions. The Book of Revelation comes to mind. If you'd like to know what's in store for the world, that's a good place to look. Chairman Mao, on the other hand, spent a lot of time talking about class struggles and politics, but he didn't appear to spend much time thinking about the end of the world.

The Bible has certain gaps, though. For example, dinosaurs that dominated the earth for 165 million years aren't mentioned. That's a difficult thing to overlook, I think. Noah's Ark would have had to be pretty large to house a brontosaurus or two. In fact, not one pair, but seven pairs of each animal were supposedly herded into the Ark. You can look it up.

Also neglected in the Bible are iPads, space shuttles, hybrid automobiles, T.V. remote controls, and, sadly, hot fudge sundaes.

No one really expects those things to be in the Bible. After all, they all arrived after the Bible was written. As for dinosaurs, perhaps we can understand the oversight, since so much of the book is devoted to more important things, like the long list of begats. I'm particularly interested in Enoch, who begat Irad, who begat Mehujael, who begat Methuselah, who begat Lamech. Nowadays, no one wants to take credit for begatting the Kardashian clan.

It's interesting to contemplate other things that are not in the Good Book. Take angels, for example. When you think of an angel, isn't the first thing you imagine a pair of wings? An angel without wings is like a lollipop without a stick. Sure, angels are described in the Bible, but their wings are not. And speaking of wings, butterflies never appear in print. That's a pity, because they would be an obvious opening for delicate beauty, which the Bible could use to help offset the ten gruesome plagues. And wouldn't a Swallowtail or two provide respite from that tedious list of begats?

The devil as we know him — with horns, goat legs, a pitchfork, red skin, and surrounded by sulfur-smelling brimstone — is not physically described, either. Our idea of hell comes mostly from Dante's Inferno.

As you may recall, Satan tempted Eve with an apple in the Garden of Eden. But the Bible doesn't exactly say "apple." It refers only to fruit. It could have been a pomegranate, a grape, or even a fig, for all we know. But I have to admit the image of Eve spitting grapefruit seeds leaves something to be desired.

Remember the whale that swallowed Jonah? Well, the Bible didn't specify a whale, actually; merely a big fish. And by the way, a whale is a mammal, not a fish. Just ask Ahab.

The Bible is the place to go for aligning your moral compass. It's pretty thorough, covering lying, stealing, and killing and 362 other forbidden commandments, like don't tattoo yourself, don't marry a harlot if you're a priest, don't have sexual relations with your father's brother's wife, and don't eat medium rare steaks. But the Bible includes no prohibition of gambling. So presumably you can gamble your house away, but don't steal a book of matches from your favorite casino, or you'll have some explaining to do in the hereafter.

Nowhere in the Bible can you find anyone praying with his or her hands folded. That idea came a lot later, maybe — I'm thinking — to discourage parishioners from picking pockets. And speaking of people helping themselves to the belongings of others, you won't find the statement, "God helps those who help themselves." That was Benjamin Franklin, God bless him, although Aesop's fables may have predated him.

The Rapture is not in the Bible, either, despite so many people who anticipate it. The concept of the Rapture was actually invented in the 1600s by Cotton Mather — the same Cotton Mather who gained notoriety for hanging women in the Salem Witch Trials. Isn't it nice to identify the individual who came up with a particular concept? You can't do that with the creator of the Internet, although a certain politician once wanted to be credited with that one.

All in all, the Bible is a complete guide to living in society. It provides a comprehensive history of people, places, and things, perhaps with the exception of Chairman Mao and velociraptors.

What the Bible Never Said

Т

he Bible is often misquoted, which gives hope to all us sinners. For example, we all know "No rest for the wicked." That quotation is derived from Isaiah 57:21, but the actual quote is "There is no peace, saith my God, to the wicked." Aha! So apparently a wicked person can get to sleep for some rest, but not peacefully.

"God helps those who help themselves" isn't found in the Bible at all, which is a pity, I think, because it would motivate my brother-in-law to get a job.

If you look in the Bible for "Pride comes before a fall," you won't find that phrase. But you might find, "Pride goeth before destruction, and an haughty spirit before a fall." Frankly, I don't know exactly how haughty my spirit has to be before my fall, but I'm not willing to take any chances, so I've resolved to reduce my haughty spirit quotient as much as possible.

Timothy, as in 1 Timothy 6:10, didn't exactly say "Money is the root of all evil." He said "the love of money is the root of all evil." It implies that you can be evil if you love money and you don't even have to have it. On the other hand, for all those who have money but don't love it, they're home free. To recap: if you don't love money, you're not evil, but you still can be wicked, in which case you won't find peace, but at least you can take a nap on a pillow of cash.

Other well-known quotations are shortened versions of the original. For example, Sir Winston Churchill could be longwinded, so we shortened, "I have nothing to offer but blood, toil, tears and sweat" simply to "blood, sweat, and tears." And of course, the musical group Blood Sweat & Tears is famous for singing the lyrics of Sir Winston: "Hi-De-Hi, Hi-De-Ho."

One of my favorite phrases is "We don't need no steenking badges!" from the film *The Treasure of the Sierra Madre*. No doubt you've used the phrase yourself on many occasions. But the phrase is only an abbreviation of the original: "Badges? We ain't got no badges! We don't need no badges. I don't have to show you any stinkin' badges!" Most of us like the shortened version better. It's easier to remember.

Speaking of movies, in *Casablanca*, Ingrid Bergman didn't say "Play it again, Sam." She said "Play it once, Sam, for old times' sake." So don't make me say that again, ma'am.

James Cagney never said "You dirty rat!" but in the movie *Blonde Crazy* he said someone is a "dirty, double-crossing rat." Much better, don't you think, especially if you have to confront a double crosser; and who doesn't from time to time?

"Win just one for the Gipper," said Pat O'Brien in *Knute Rockne, All American*. But we remember the phrase more mellifluously and simply as "Win one for the Gipper."

Although Tom Hanks in the movie *Apollo 13* said "Houston, we have a problem," actually Astronaut Jack Swigert radioed, "Houston, we've had a problem here." By using the past perfect tense, Swigert implied a problem once existed but it didn't anymore, which could have misled the Apollo Mission Control Center. That wouldn't be the way I would have phrased it, but luckily for the manned space program, I was never invited to participate.

Oliver Hardy didn't tell Stan Laurel, "Well, here's another fine mess you've gotten me into." He said "Well, here's another nice mess you've gotten me into!" Maybe you have to be Stan or Ollie to fully appreciate the subtle distinction.

Remember Mae West's line in *She Done Him Wrong*? It was "Is that a gun in your pocket, or are you just happy to see me?" But it doesn't appear in that or any of her movies. It was too risqué back in 1933.

In *Jaws*, the famous line, "We're gonna need a bigger boat!" was actually "You're gonna need a bigger boat!" Roy Scheider tried to distance himself from the danger of a shark attack, as I would have, but it didn't work for poor Quint, the boat's owner.

Surprisingly, in the film *Algiers*, and as much as we could swear to the contrary, Charles Boyer never said to Hedy Lamarr, "Come with me to the Casbah."

On the other hand, I think you'll agree "'Step into my parlor,' said the spider to the fly" sounds better than the original quote, "Will you walk into my parlor?"

Bela Lugosi, a/k/a Dracula, never said "I want to suck your blood!" Now that's disappointing. I'll have to use another phrase to scare the kiddies at Halloween.

By now, we all know "That's one small step for a man, one giant leap for mankind" wasn't received accurately on earth due to static. You have to feel sorry for Neil Armstrong who probably practiced that line a hundred times before he took that first step on the moon.

When it comes to plays, William Congreve in *The Mourning Bride*, didn't write "Music hath charms to soothe the savage beast," but the savage breast. Nicer image, don't you think? And I'm not just saying that because I'm a guy.

George Bernard Shaw never said "England and America are two countries divided by a common language," but Oscar Wilde came close in *The Canterville Ghost*: "We really have everything in common with America nowadays except, of course, language."

Carl Sagan said "there are maybe 100 billion galaxies and 10 billion trillion stars." Only Johnny Carson said "billions and billions."

"For one thing," Sagan explained, "it's too imprecise."

It wasn't George Washington who said "I cannot tell a lie. It was I who chopped down the cherry tree." It was Parson Weems, one of his biographers, who made it up. Really changes your sterling impression of our first president, right?

Here's one that Albert Einstein may have said. "The definition of insanity is doing the same thing over and over and expecting different results." The quote seems accurate, but we don't know if it was Einstein or Ben Franklin who said it first.

Mark Twain never said, "Whenever I feel the urge to exercise, I lie down until it goes away." But it sure sounds like him. Here's a quotation he did first say: take it easy. Yes, Mr. Twain. Always good advice.

The phrase most famously associated with Cary Grant, "Judy, Judy, Judy" was never spoken by Grant in a movie. But later he did admit, "I improve on misquotation." I know what he's saying. I, myself, thrive on misquotation.

Did Marie Antoinette say, "Let them eat cake?" No. But since that's her most famous quotation, I'm willing to let it slide with no grain of salt.

Words You Can't Live Without

I've got just a few more words for you today, words you won't be able to live without or, as Winston Churchill might have said, "words without which you would be hard pressed to exist."

Once you hear these words and, of course, use them as frequently as Winston might have, they'll become part of you, tripping off your tongue at every opportunity, and you'll wonder how you got along without them.

The first one is omphaloskepsis, or the contemplation of one's navel. Suppose you work in an office with cubicles and your neighboring cubicle dweller is staring down, as many Asperger patients do, in the general direction of his shoelaces. This is how you might use your new word in a sentence. You might say, "Hey, Fred, I see you're practicing omphaloskepsis, but don't worry, I won't tell the boss. I wouldn't want to provoke his trichotillomania."

Ah, trichotillomania. That's the abnormal desire to pull out one's hair. The statement won't work, of course, if the boss is already bald, but admit it: it's almost impossible to pass up an opportunity to use omphaloskepsis and trichotillomania in the same sentence, isn't it?

Now let's just say you're going to lunch with Fred, after he's had time to google and digest the new words you've shared with him. And let's say you and Fred come upon a young, attractive mother with perfectly coiffed hair, impeccable makeup, and a figure right out of a magazine that you wouldn't find in a dentist's office; she's in a stylishly short skirt and 7" high heels and she is pushing a stroller crammed with infant twins to whom she coos breathlessly a la Marilyn Monroe.

You might blurt out, "Madam, for the love of God, it's unseemly to broadcast your polyphiloprogenitive tendencies for the world to observe." I would expect you to receive a rather embarrassed look from the woman and, of course, a subdued snicker from Fred at your side. That's assuming, of course, that both Fred and Miss November realize polyphiloprogenitive means extremely prolific, tending to produce offspring. Actually, anyone seen in public with more than one offspring would be fair game for chiding like that, don't you think?

Here's another word that you'll use as often as a politician says, "The American people want." It's myrmecophilous, or associated with ants. For example, if on your way back to the office after lunch, your buddy Fred with full-blown Asperger's Syndrome makes a show of sidestepping to avoid an anthill, I suspect you would automatically accuse him of blatant myrmecophilousity.

"Ha ha, Fred," you might say, or words to that effect, "I've rarely seen an instance of more blatant myrmecophilousity. Pull yourself together, man. People are beginning to stare."

Do be careful, however, Fred doesn't mistake your gentle rebuke as coming from a psychotomimetic, one who induces psychotic behavior in others. After all, Fred may be the most well-balanced friend you have and you'll need him if you plan to let loose more 50¢ words in the future, quick as a hemidemisemiquaver, or sixty-fourth note.

TECHNOBABBLE

All I Really Need to Know I Learned on Facebook

In 1986, Robert Fulghum wrote a book entitled *All I Really Need to Know I Learned in Kindergarten*. It's an interesting book — light reading, seeing the world through the eyes of a child. It contains moral lessons, like don't speak with your mouth full. Learn how to share. Buy low, sell high. But that is so 20th century.

Now we have Facebook. This is an online social network. Let me take a step backward to tell you how it works.

You all know about computers, those electronic marvels that you can't live without. They're in your car, your TV, and probably in your wristwatch. By the way, computers were never predicted by science fiction writers before they were invented. That's an interesting factoid, since just about everything else, like space ships, radar, robots, and laser beams, WERE predicted, not by Newton or Einstein, but by science fiction writers like Heinlein and Asimov.

Anyway, we know about computers. Many of us have seen them; some of us even own a desktop, a laptop, or a PDA — personal digital assistant, like an iPhone. And a few of us know about the Internet and email, which makes it more or less easy to communicate with other people from the comfort of your keyboard. It's not as easy as the telephone, but at least the other party can't interrupt you, while you're conveying your message, with a story about their damn grandkids' soccer game.

When you send an electronic mail or email message, it arrives at the recipient's computer through some sort of magic and it waits there until the recipient feels like reading it on his or her computer. So, you see where it got its name: e-MAIL.

There are some drawbacks to email, though. One is that you can correspond with only a limited number of people at a time, and only if you know their email addresses. An electronic address, by the way, is a series of letters and numbers that has an encircled "a" sign in it.

This was a nice way to reintroduce the "at" sign to younger generations, since nothing is ever sold singly any more. You can't buy a single screw in a hardware store, for instance, like the old days: one screw @ 3¢. But I digress.

Oh, one more digression: Supreme Court Justice Felix Frankfurter's wife said that there were only two things wrong with Felix's speeches. He digressed from his text; and he returned to it.

These digressions to digressions show that I've been reading too much Stephen King. Back to my slender thread.

So along came Facebook in February, 2004, exclusively for Harvard students, similar to MySpace a year before it, and hundreds of other social networks after, with names we're all familiar with: Twitter, Plurk, Capazoo, Cloob, and Mixi, for example. Within two weeks of its introduction, half of the Harvard student body had joined Facebook. And within a few months, 30 other colleges were part of the network.

After all, Harvard is located in Massachusetts, where you can't throw a stone without hitting a college student. So, it was logical for Facebook to start with students at Harvard.

Facebook is no longer a social network just for college students; 11% of its users are over the age of 35, and the fastest growing demographic? People over 30.

Think of it like radio. It's a cultural phenomenon that buzzes along invisibly, under the surface of our perception, like blood flowing through our tired old arteries.

If you don't have a radio, you don't know what Rush Limbaugh is angry about this week. Likewise, if you're not on Facebook, you're missing a flow of information that may be almost as important as Rush's rantings, which isn't saying much.

Facebook is now the largest of the online social networks internationally, with more than one billion members or contributors or whatever you call them. It adds 200,000 new people every workday — a million new users per week.

It grew so large that its founder, Mark Zuckerberg, turned down an offer by Yahoo in 2006 to buy the company for $1 billion. He became known as the kid who turned down a billion. I saw a recent picture of him. He still looks like a kid. But someday he'll turn 30 and then he may have a better appreciation for what he's created, to say nothing of what he could do with $1 billion.

Microsoft owns a small percentage of the Face-book company now, ostensibly to keep Google away.

The company is now valued at about $15 billion, which makes it the fifth most valuable U.S. Internet company. Ahh, the power of intellectual property. But Facebook's revenue is only (ONLY!) $150 million per year. That's only 1% of its value.

But back to the social network concept. Online social networks said, "Why not provide a system that allows a few or a great number of people to see each other's messages? And while we're at it, why not include photographs and videos?" In fact, Facebook is now the largest repository of photographs.

Over three billion photos are accessed by users every day and it adds 60 million photos to its database every week.

This reminds me: you can use obscenities in your messages, but you can't post naked or obscene photos. I've heard other web sites specialize in that.

So, the idea is you post some information on Facebook and you let other people see and comment on that information. Your information can be as detailed and formerly private as you wish.

You can mention what you do for a living, where you live, and — only God knows why you'd want to — even your weight. Hey grandparents: you can finally show off pictures — many pictures — of your grand-children!

By the same token, you can visit other people's Facebook page and comment on their information or even make fun of their grandchildren.

For example, I might say that I dislike cats and I aim for them when I'm in my car. That's sure to elicit comments from the people who see my statement.

They're called friends — people who are linked to my Facebook page. Some of my "friends" can be a bit nasty to me. It is not unusual to find people who have hundreds of friends on Facebook. One of my friends has 1,500 other friends, but she's selling tea and she posts lovely photos of herself wearing a bikini. I'm not sure it's the tea that is the main attraction to her Facebook page.

Of course, that's nothing compared to Susan Boyle, the middle-aged Scottish woman who impressed the judges on Britain's Got Talent.

She attracted over a million members to her Facebook fan club in barely a week.

I've found some people with 5,000 friends. That's like the size of Binghamton in another 10 years.

I joined Facebook a few years ago. Did I mention that it's free? As one of the oldest members of Facebook, I'd like to share some of my observations with you.

First of all, by seeing my friends' profiles, which are like resumes, I now realize that I am the only being on this planet who does not own at least one cat.

In fact, some people don't bother to post a photo of themselves on their profile; their cats are there, instead.

Users are encouraged to list their birthday on their profile page. Fortunately, you can get away with your birth month and day and omit your birth year. There's a birthday calendar that reminds you when one of your friends is about to celebrate a birthday, so you can send him a customized electronic birthday card. The next time your birthday comes around, imagine how nice it would be to receive, say, 2,000 birthday greetings online.

I also noticed, by reviewing my friends' photos, that I am virtually alone in never having posed for a picture with a glass or bottle containing an alcoholic beverage. Frankly, some of the imbibers on Facebook don't look like they're old enough to drink. In fact, almost none of them do.

But not to be outdone, I am preparing to upload a photograph showing me holding a cup and a bottle of Geritol to indicate my age, in case my lack of hairline doesn't give it away.

I've embarked on another Facebook project, as a matter of fact. I thought it would be nice to make online friends who were more attractive than my real-life friends. So I started to find tiny thumbnail images of good-looking people — young women, to be exact — dressed in the sort of beachwear Golda Meir wouldn't have approved of.

95

Most of these very young ladies live near Hollywood and are named Tiffany or Ashley or Summer; but some of them are in Italy, apparently near beaches. They have names like Rosita, Lucia and Emanuela.

Turns out, many bikini-clad women have bikini-clad friends. Who knew? My project was a lot easier than I had expected. The bottom line is that I haven't met or spoken with 90% of my Facebook friends. In fact, we don't even speak the same language. But those whom I haven't met sure look sexy.

Some of the Facebook profile photos have two or more people in them, so I sometimes don't know what my friend actually looks like. I always assume she's the one in the bikini.

Much older people — and I'm talking about 40-year-olds — tend to use photos of themselves that were taken 10 or 20 years ago. My brother-in-law did that and I could barely recognize him.

From the messages I've seen that are sent to and from other Facebook members, I can tell that, by far, the main activity of high school and college kids is attending parties. They're absolutely obsessed with that activity.

I suppose that's no surprise to their parents, but it's one area that we don't share an interest. I absolutely HATE parties, you see. I find them superficial and pretentious. That may be exactly why young people like them so much.

You can list your religious persuasion on Facebook and many people do.

I was surprised to see how many people state they are spiritual or they believe in God, but do not ascribe to an organized religion.

I was thinking about how many friends Moses would have, if he were on Facebook today. In his profile, he could say he had leadership qualities. His hobbies could include parting the Red Sea.

And the Moses profile photo could show him only 90 years old with a bottle of Manischewitz.

Online social networks like Facebook have modified the theory that each of us is no more than 6 degrees of separation from any person on the planet. In other words, through a chain of acquaintances, you can be connected to anyone.

For example, you know me and I know Mr. Jones and he knows Mr. Brown and he knows Mr. Kevin Bacon and he knows Carla Bruni-Sarkozy, French President Nicolas Sarkozy's wife who, coincidentally, is all over the Internet wearing nothing but her Chanel No. 5.

As more and more people become connected to a social network and to each other, it will be easier for anyone to locate anyone.

That is the principle behind the 300-million-member web site, LinkedIn, which allows a job seeker to locate a job. He can discover the path by which he can communicate with the employer through a mutual, trusted contact. LinkedIn is acquiring one new member every second.

So you see, socializing through technology is a growing phenomenon. More and more web sites are dedicated to finding friends or a mate. The site called J-Date, like e-Harmony, allows Jewish people to find each other from the comfort of their home. Your popularity is measured by the number of online friends you have.

Even before Facebook, my former boss at IBM would spend days on end in his office with his door closed, emailing me, along with the rest of his underlings, rather than crossing the hallway that separated our offices. We all thought he was anti-social. But it turns out he was 20 years ahead of his time, and anti-social.

The younger generation is becoming more e-human. I wonder whether they will lose the ability to converse, person-to-person. Will they be content to toast each other with booze in front of their computers, instead of in more healthy ways at more conventional places, like in smoky bars?

Automatic Men's Rooms

Have you experienced those automatic toilets in men's rooms and I suppose, now that I think of it, in women's rooms? They're the ones that know when you're finished doing your business and they flush without your having to touch the lever. They're installed on urinals, too.

It's the most amazing invention since indoor plumbing, if you ask me. Sometimes, though, you stand up to stretch and they flush before you actually finish. And once, the automatic toilet didn't flush for me even though I stood up, so I sat down again and stood up.

Nothing happened.

Then I waved my hand in front of the sensor.

No luck.

As far as I could see, there was no emergency override button to push for just such situations. So, I sat down again with all of my clothes on, feeling foolish, and I got to my feet again.

Finally, it flushed.

I believe it was trying to embarrass me, but the joke was on the toilet. After all, I was the only one in the stall, so no one else knew about my silly shenanigans — until just now, that is.

When you exit your stall, you find the sink, of course. Some sinks now have their own sensor. Water comes on and shuts itself off when you move your hands in and out of the sink. You can't adjust the temperature, but that's such a small price to pay for advanced technology.

A soap dispenser can also be automatic. Same story. But if you're as impatient as I've been known to be, you might pull your hand away just before that last drop of soap is dispensed, wasting that drop at the edge of the sink and making you hope the dispenser doesn't report back to that big soap reservoir in the sky.

The real problem arises when the faucet is automatic but the soap dispenser isn't. Then you have to push down on the soap dispenser physically and pump it to get it to work. What's with that? Either the bathroom is automated or it's not, right?

Believe me, I enjoy futilely waving my hand in front of a soap dispenser while other people are standing in line behind me as much as anyone. But there comes a time when choreography becomes a pointless exercise. You don't know if the thing is out of soap — in which case you can shift to the adjacent sink — or if you're inadvertently dealing with a manual pumping dispenser à la the 18th century.

I recently entered a men's room that had a big circular contraption, about four feet wide, between the door and the toilet stalls. At first, I thought I might have to use what could be a communal urinal, but it quickly dawned on me that the contraption was just a large sink. Whew. So far, so good.

I wonder how many guys are fooled into unzipping in front of what looked like a satellite antenna urinal.

But as I approached the contraption to rinse my hands, nothing happened.

I started to wave my hand, both hands, in fact.

Still nothing.

Luckily, a gentleman was nearby, fussing with an automatic paper towel dispenser.

What an idiot, I could imagine him thinking. He had that pitying look that my grandmother reserved for certain inept underlings. She even had a Hungarian word for it: *sagan*. It means *poor thing*.

What he said was, "Buddy, just step on the bar under the sink and the water will flow."

I guess more embarrassing things can happen in the men's room than requesting help at a sink, but most humiliating events seem to happen to me in public, unfamiliar restrooms.

When you finally figure out the weird, oversized faucet and sink and you rinse your hands, you approach the paper towel dispenser. Here we go again. Some of them are automatic and begin to eject a sheet of paper when your wet hand approaches them. But some extend part of a roll of paper. Am I the only one who resents having to grasp the sheet with my wet hands from the otherwise automatic paper dispenser? If it's smart enough to sense your hand and eject paper, shouldn't it be smart enough to cut the paper, so you don't have to rip it from the machine?

Of course, one sheet of paper is rarely enough. Your hand can still be damp and you don't want to exit the restroom like that.

What if you bump into someone outside, like your stockbroker, and he offers you his hand to shake? You can see his expression when he meets you, just out of the men's room, and shakes your damp hand. You're forced to apologize, explaining, "No, it's not what you think; it's just water."

Here's the situation: you haven't seen the fellow in four months, your stock portfolio is taking a dive, he never returns your desperate calls, and all you can talk about is the source of your wet hand. He doesn't really believe you, anyway.

Okay, so you will need a second sheet of paper, either to finish the hand-drying job or to stockpile some paper for the trip home. You wave your hand in front of the damn automatic paper dispenser a second time. But the machine knows the first sheet should be enough, especially if you have small hands and you already shook them vigorously over the sink, or you rinsed only one of them, or it's thinking maybe you'll give up after the first sheet if it waits long enough to dispense another one. Sometimes you have to wait 8 or 10 seconds before it will give you a second sheet.

Who has time for that, when your stockbroker, Sagan, is outside waiting to shake your hand?

Bad Designs

It strikes me that the people who design things may not always use those things themselves. That's certainly true of computer keyboards and, before that, typewriter keyboards. In fact, the story I heard was that the original typewriter keyboard designer intentionally laid out the keys so that accomplished touch typists would have to slow down, thus ensuring that they wouldn't jam the keys. We are basically stuck with the old keys layout even though computer keyboards don't jam. But modern designers still thwart good typists by inserting control, alt, and command keys in the way of the shift and shift lock keys. The most prolific keyboard designers are probably hunt and peck typists.

Controls for cars aren't always intuitive, either. I had an S.U.V. for a couple of years once and I never did get used to the driver's controls. Every time I tried to turn on the right blinker, the windshield wipers started acting up. It was only when it started to rain, usually at night, that I couldn't figure out how to turn the wipers on. And as if the windshield wiper/turn signal post weren't crowded enough, some designer added headlight controls to them. Every function but the one I want gets activated.

Sometimes the four-way flasher button is so well hidden, I have to resort to the owner's manual. And changing the clock for daylight savings time? I've been known to be patient for six months until the world caught up with my clock.

Nowadays cell phones all seem to be different. The same key that connects a call on one phone disconnects a call on another one. Or makes my conversation a three-way conference exactly when that causes the greatest embarrassment. I wonder if there's some sort of competition among designers to inconvenience customers the most.

The ultimate consumer devices will be completely unusable. We can all look forward to that day.

Can't Wait for Self-Driving Cars

You've probably heard about self-driving cars and trucks. These are vehicles of the near future that will be almost totally automatic, driving themselves without help from their slightly shell-shocked passengers. No one will be steering or, more importantly, applying the brakes, unless those people want to meet that big chauffer in the sky.

The way they work, I understand, is by bouncing locations and directions off satellites, the way GPS systems work now. The difference is that, in addition to knowing where I am and how to get to where I want to go, my self-driving car will actually get me to my destination while I read a book or look out the window or have an argument with my child on my cell phone or doze off altogether, like I've been known to do even while driving my Edsel.

These cars are supposed to avoid getting into accidents with other cars or motorcycles or pedestrians. And they're supposed to stop at every red light and stop sign, both talents that I'm still working on after all these years.

And there will be no risk of banging into anything when backing out of a parking space at the supermarket. How cool is that? Maybe it will know when I'm about to run out of gas or when I need an oil change. And maybe it will take me to a service station that charges less for gas than the guys who usually rip me off. It will no doubt get better gas mileage than I do, but that's not saying much.

I expect my self-driving car will know when it's raining so it will turn on my windshield wipers. And it will know when the sun goes down, so it can turn on my headlights, although maybe it won't need to have clear windshields or headlights at all, now that I think of it. It will be that smart.

And it will handle itself better in snow than I do, but that's not saying much.

I'm hoping it will avoid pot-holes and will know, in advance, where the speed traps are, so I don't get a speeding ticket when we're doing, say, 35 miles over the limit. Of course, if a cop does stop me, I can always blame the speed on the software that's controlling my car, sort of like I explain to my wife when I'm listening to Rossini on the radio.

All in all, I'm really looking forward to owning a self-

AT THE NEXT INTERSECTION, TAKE A LEFT...

driving car of the future. But I think I'll wait to buy one that can cook a pizza.

Fooled in TV Land

In 1978, I moved into a small, one-story ranch house in Queens. That moving day was unusually warm in September, as I recall, so I opened the windows in every room. As I soon learned, the new house was only a few miles from LaGuardia Airport, directly in the flight path of approaching aircraft.

The movers had already unloaded and placed most of the furniture in respective rooms. All that was left was to unpack boxes. I had just unloaded a number of heavy boxes of books and, unaccustomed to physical exertion as I was — and as I still am, in fact — I decided to rest a bit before continuing the mindless task of unpacking. So I switched on the TV and plopped myself on the unmade bed for a short rest.

The TV happened to be showing a United Air Lines commercial, culminating in a jet taking off into a very blue sky. From that image, I knew the jet was not flying in my new neighborhood, which is normally covered by a low ceiling of milky clouds the local weather forecasters insist on calling "partly sunny." No, the deep blue sky in the airline commercial looked like it was over Yellowstone or the Grand Canyon or some exotic place so pollution free I thought this must be the first airplane ever to fly over it.

As the plane took off smoothly in the TV commercial, a pleasant jingle played and an announcer implored me to fly United. I heard a crescendo of music and jet engines, too. In fact, the sound of the engines eventually drowned out the announcer's voice.

The next event really surprised me. The volume of the engines increased and increased, even as the commercial faded out and the Jerry Springer Show resumed. And then my windows started to rattle.

"Wow," I thought, "this is one realistic airline commercial. It's sensorama. I can still hear and feel the engines long after the TV image is gone. My bedroom feels like it's in an earthquake. How did they do that?"

That's when it occurred to me that the sound was no longer coming from the TV. Jet engines were overhead. I felt foolish, not only because I thought the TV could shake my windows, but because I realized I had purchased a house that would force me to experience this thrill every few minutes, summer after summer.

It is now about 30 years later. I no longer live in Queens. I have a large, flat screen TV with an auxiliary sound system, including expensive speakers that the sales person told me would make the difference between merely viewing television programs and actually living them.

"You'll hear the crashing of football helmets, Dude," he enthused, "like you were on the field with the players." I raised my eyebrows. "Singers will sound like they're in the same room with you, Bud. Car chase scenes and NASCAR races will make you reach for your seatbelt, Sparky. You just have to have this X-3000 Super Sound System, amigo. There's no sense having a large screen TV with little, wimpy speakers. It really defeats the purpose, don't you think? Go with the X-3000 Triple S, Bro. Take it from me: you'll never regret it."

"Okay," I said. "I'll buy it."

I don't live near an airport anymore, I'm happy to report, but the place where I reside is fairly open. If the TV is playing in the living room, I can hear it in the kitchen and in the hallway and in the spare bedroom for what I hoped would be my office and private sanctuary.

Sometimes when I'm not watching the set, I hear a siren that sounds like it's right outside. I can't resist looking out the window for the ambulance. The sound from my TV is realistic enough for me to think a police car is about to crash through to my condo on the 26th floor.

When a telephone rings in a TV program, it causes me to hunt for my cell phone. This is most embarrassing when friends are visiting, especially when I have to ask them to stand up so I can search under couch cushions for my phone.

Frankly, I'm concerned that if my condo ever does start burning, I'll lose precious time racing around the place through the billowing smoke, turning off TVs instead of preparing to be rescued.

Today, none of us is taken in by the scratchy, blurry sounds of 1914 Charlie Chaplin movies or of Orson Welles's 1938 radio broadcast of the War of the Worlds. I suppose in a hundred years people might be amazed at how unsophisticated we were in the early 21st century, when the X-3000 was able to fool us.

All I can say is my TV does too good a job convincing me that the sounds I hear are real. And the high definition sight of Fritos, Cheetos, and potato chips dancing across my screen prevents me from switching off the set long enough to escape back into reality.

Inventors are My Heroes

When did inventors get the reputation of being crackpots and weirdoes? Ironically, they brought it on themselves with their own inventions. Hoist, as it were, by their own widgets.

A hundred years ago, everyone knew the superstar inventors of the day: Tom Edison, Alexander Graham Bell, Henry Ford, Charles Goodyear, Harvey Firestone, and John Kellogg, to name a few. But along came movies and radio and then TV, along with celebrities singing and dancing their way into our hearts... or into the hearts of our grandparents. They sang, they danced, and they acted on horseback, and in hospitals, and on good ship lollipops, and got carried by big apes to the top of the Empire State Building. They fought Klingons in galaxies far, far away.

Add to them sports figures, rock stars, billionaires, and politicians, news anchor persons, talk show hosts, and stand-up comedians. It seemed like overnight, famous inventors were eclipsed by the American Idol nueveaux popular.

Today, most of us can't name five famous living inventors. I can't do it and I'm in the invention business. The very mention of the word, inventor, brings to mind wild-eyed, unkempt, absent-minded old men with hair disheveled and expressions insane, like Albert Einstein the moment he grabbed a high voltage power line.

It's not that inventors have all disappeared. Our generation has been introduced to their recent inventions, like personal computers, iPods, GPS devices, cell phones, satellite radio, barcode scanners, Pop-Tarts, MRI machines, compact discs, air bags, and digital thermo-meters. But it's anonymous teams of corporate inventors who are responsible for those little ditties... no match for Britneys and Tigers and Nicoles and Madonnas.

So the inventor, like the noble dinosaur, has been relegated to a quaint footnote in history... an unfortunate fate worsened by dint of the ridicule heaped upon him.

When I see a characterization of a wacko inventor in a movie, like Christopher Lloyd in Back to the Future, I become so upset that only a strawberry Pop-Tart can calm me.

Instant Gratification

I used to live in Florida with my wife, my puppy Cashew, and my books. A lot of books. So many books, in fact, I sought a one-bedroom condo with an attached library, but apparently that's not a popular configuration for Florida condos.

In order to accommodate my 33 bookcases, I had to locate a large condo, one with five bedrooms. And even then, it was a tight squeeze. Along with the five bedrooms came six bathrooms. That's three bathrooms each for my wife and me. Cashew didn't show much interest in indoor plumbing.

For reasons I won't describe now, and frankly that I can't justify, I recently decided to move to Colorado. We began to hunt for a house here and discovered (alas!) the same irrational prejudice against serious book collectors. There are simply no one-bedroom libraries for sale in Colorado, as far as I can see.

By now, the collection of books I can't live without had increased, so a measly five-bedroom house wouldn't do. I'll return to this state of affairs shortly.

While waiting to find a suitable Colorado mansion, my wife, my puppy, and I reserved an extended stay motel in Colorado. The books were packed neatly in 300 cardboard cartons and stored in what our moving agent called a secure location somewhere between the Atlantic Ocean and the Rocky Mountains. The extended stay motel had a miniscule kitchen, a tiny living room, and a bedroom barely large enough to contain our bed.

Oh yes, it was outfitted with a modest bathroom, too. You can imagine the hardship my wife and I had to endure to deal with a single bathroom after leaving our former, spacious Florida condo. Now, 2,000 miles from the Atlantic, all I had to view while waiting for the bathroom to be available was the snow-capped Rocky Mountain range.

As I mentioned, during the time I was in Florida, my library grew. More books equates to more bookcases and, therefore, more bedrooms and more bathrooms, since Americans are passionate about plumbing fixtures. We just purchased a lovely place significantly larger than the condo. So far, so good.

But wait, as they say on infomercials, there's more. The bathroom saga has not ended. Instead of the six bathrooms we had taken for granted, our new place now has eight of them. That, alone, would represent an impressive improvement in our living situation. But it's even better than that. One of our bathrooms is actually located in the garage. How convenient is that? Brilliant! That will be the high point of tours I conduct through my new house. I have to wonder why every house doesn't have a bathroom in its garage.

I wouldn't say I'm obsessing over toilets, but it's certainly one of the topics I contemplate from my throne when I'm not, you know, reading a book.

It's About Time

It wasn't so long ago that we humans didn't keep track of time very well. Oh sure, our ancestors knew when spring was arriving and approximately when to plant corps. And they knew, by the phases of the moon, when to celebrate certain holidays. But specific, lesser durations of time like hours and minutes didn't seem to matter to them.

"Really," I can hear them saying, "what difference does it make whether we plant the corn at 10:15 or 11:33 this year?"

In 1492, the dialogue might have gone:

"Oh, Ferdinand, want to sale our ship to the edge of the world?"

"Count me in, Chris. When do we leave?"

"When the wind picks up and we've loaded all the Spanish doubloons."

Even the most sociopathic but least organized of our ancestors could have said, "Don't forget: tomorrow, when Attila and the rest of his gang arrive, we'll start to pillage the town."

Such inexact estimates of time worked perfectly well for humans before we knew any better.

It wasn't until the 15th century that spring-driven clocks became accurate enough to keep track of hours and minutes. And it wasn't until the 17th century that pendulum clocks made their appearance. Atomic clocks, of course, didn't arrive until the 20th century. So, you see, very accurate timepieces are a relatively recent development.

Yet in the last six centuries, look how well we've adapted to accurate time measurements. We don't say, "I'll meet you sometime for lunch tomorrow." We say, "I'll meet you at Uncle Butch's Sushi-rama at 12:30 sharp."

Nor do we plan on boarding a flight to Cleveland by telling our spouse to meet at the airport with a vague deadline like, "before the day gets too warm." Instead, we say, "It's a 1:47 flight, so let's leave the house by 11:50."

And of course, we don't advise each other to tune in to Thursday Night Football when it starts to get dark outside. That sort of imprecision nowadays could lead to missing the kickoff and maybe a 129-yard runback score.

What most of us live by today are precise schedules monitored by perfect time instruments. If I don't pick up my daughter from ballet school on time and she's freezing outside the building in nothing but her tutu, I can't blame my wristwatch. I think excuses used to be easier to come by before the Industrial Revolution.

We've also adapted to shorter and shorter time periods, unlike the people before us. Did biblical farmers have a snooze button on their alarm clocks like my friend Ruth, to catch another seven minutes of rest before starting to plow? And did Neanderthals wrestle with a decision about how many twelve-minute intervals to pay for at the parking meter before they ran into a pizzeria for a slice?

It was not only impossible to measure time so accurately in the past, but unnecessary unless the Marie Antoinette's three-minute egg was in danger of overcooking again and her cook's head was on the line.

Now it's not only time that is measured so accurately. It could be distance, too. When was the last time someone gave you directions to a location by saying, "it's down the road apiece" or "go west for a while and you'll see the joint on your right?" Our GPS devices tell us exactly how far we are from our destination and they predict our arrival time with breathtaking accuracy.

Speed limits are posted precisely, unlike composers who suggested speeds for their musical compositions with words that translated to "very slow," "moderately slow," "at a walking pace," "moderately fast," and "lively." Imagine if speed limit signs on our interstates used suggestive words like that.

Even our messages to each other are shortened, when texting or tweeting. I can't fathom Shakespeare squeezing Hamlet's soliloquy into 140 characters. If that were the case, the audience would never have fully appreciated Hamlet's dilemma about whether life was worth living.

If Lincoln drastically truncated the Gettysburg's Address like that, people wouldn't know whether our government of the people, by the people, for the people would perish from the earth. Goodness! Think of all the term papers that wouldn't have been written in the ensuing seven score and ten years.

The bottom line is we're all dealing with shorter and shorter fuses. Many of you may welcome the time, in fact, when Levy's essays will be shorter than it takes our NPR host, Robert Conrad, to introduce them.

J.I.R.

What do you think about that Journal of Irreproducible Results? What? Never heard of it? Well, you're not alone. Even though it was started over 50 years ago and is published quarterly, most people have never seen an issue. It's not on many newsstands. Its print run is barely 1,000.

The Journal of Irreproducible Results — say that fast five times; I dare you. I'll just call it the J.I.R. The J.I.R. is a sort of Mad Magazine that appeals mostly to scientists — or at least scientists who have a sense of humor. That places it in a niche category, I guess. It includes all sorts of pseudo technical articles, poems, photographs and cartoons most appreciated by scientists or engineers or physicians.

For example, here are some titles of published articles:

"Calculating the Velocity of Darkness"

"Why Lectures Seem to Last Forever"

"The Fly-powered Airplane"

"Deep Space Hand Salutes"

"Chickens in Space"

"Medical Handwriting Course: Illegibility 201"

"Acoustic Oscillations in Jell-O with and without Fruit"

"Thermodynamic Study of Ultra-cold Jellybeans"

"Saucepans under Observation Never Reach a Phase Transition"

"Mushroom Hunting for Beginners"

I happen to be on the editorial board for the J.I.R., so of course I'm biased about the quality.

A few years ago, my study was published titled, "The Proliferation of Traffic Signaling Devices on the Vestal Parkway." Based on my observation that traffic lights continue to multiply over time, I was able to predict when every intersection in America would have its own traffic light and even when every driveway would have one.

After consuming a fair number of animal crackers a few years ago, I also submitted a paper to the J.I.R. titled, "Perverse Depictions in Otherwise Innocuous Foodstuffs." This included certain animal crackers that were attached to each other in suggestive ways. I provided photographs of inter-species animals in compromising positions to illustrate my study. You know: side-to-side, front-to-front, front-to-back. That sort of thing. Once again, though, this is radio, so you'll have to use your imagination.

When I'm introduced as a speaker, I usually include some J.I.R. factoid in my bio, so I can stump the person who introduces me. It's not easy to say "irreproducible" the first time. Try it yourself. I'll wait.

If you're in the market for a present for the scientist in your life who has everything, consider a subscription to the Journal of Irreproducible Results. If nothing else, it will be fun to hear him try to pronounce it.

Joke Delays on the Internet

Has this happened to you? Someone starts to tell you a joke and you realize you've heard it before.

Well that happens ten times more frequently with email. Here's why: you don't have to see another person or even call him on the phone to hear a joke. There's really no limit to how many folks can contact you by email at the same time with the same once-humorous story.

Email is used to relay jokes and funny pictures and cartoons more often than for just about any other purpose. Cyberspace must be pretty much filled up with jokes. It must be an LOL riot out there.

And it's not only jokes and photos that make the rounds. You see the same YouTube movies, too, over and over and over.

The good news is that now you don't have to be polite to your computer, like you do to your old Uncle Nat. You can just quit or delete the email halfway through. You can be as abrupt as you wish you could be with relatives.

Speaking of being abrupt, I occasionally hear from someone who lets me know he or she heard the joke already. They can't resist saying "that's an old one" or "I heard that one already." Sheesh! I took the trouble to forward the joke. Couldn't they be gracious enough not to respond? Can't they just LIG — let it go?

It's rare to hear an awfully old joke recited in a conversation, but it happens all the time with email. I still can't understand that. Electronic messages travel at the speed of light, even if you're a slow typist. Shouldn't jokes reach every connected person around the world in minutes or hours? Surely within a day. And yet I get jokes by email that are 14 months old.

What we need is some way to let people know we've seen or heard the joke before, without insulting them by actually sending a response. Maybe a bored, smiley face icon would work.

Kid Inventors: General

For the last quarter century, I've been involved with the New York State Invention Convention program for students between kindergarten and eighth grade. Some 20,000 youngsters have participated in the student invention program, creating invention models from mousetraps to ozone layer repair kits.

One kindergarten student lamented the lack of mud during hot summer days, mud being the main ingredient in mud pies, as it happens. So the five-year-old inventor mounted an inverted bottle of water and one filled with dirt onto the bathroom wall. Now he can concoct a batch of mud in the comfort of his parents' bathtub.

Speaking of homes, one student was faced with the problem of walking his dog every afternoon. He invented a virtual reality helmet for his pet that can now walk around the living room imagining it is encountering fields, flowers, and, of course, fire hydrants. Perhaps the inventor, like Alfred Nobel, can be excused for not anticipating unintended consequences of the invention.

The youngest children, having less science and engineering education and being less worldly, tend to ignore the details that would make their inventions enabling, as patent examiners are fond of saying. The youngest kids often invent machines consisting of push buttons: "a button to make me pretty"; "a button to mow my lawn"; or "a button to groom my horse." One second grader invented a "Wishing Pill" to be ingested prior to making a wish. Once the pill is swallowed, she said, "then it will come true." Another second grader invented a "Dream Maker" hat with a dial to select the type of dream he desired. He suggested four categories: good dream, bad dream, no dream, or random dream.

A seventh grader created the single invention that appealed to most adults over the years. His grandfather was stopped for speeding by a police officer. The observant grandson noticed the officer requested Grandpa's license and registration. But suddenly an urgent radio call directed the officer to the scene of a hold up. The officer told Grandpa he had no time to write the speeding ticket. As the frustrated officer prepared to leave, he warned Grandpa to slow down. It seemed a logical step for this student inventor to devise a radar detector-shaped electronic box for the dashboard. When stopped for speeding, Grandpa can now push a button that generates a radio signal to call the cop somewhere else.

One student decided to "fix the hole in the ozone layer" by creating a patch that astronauts could sew onto the remaining ozone.

The bathroom represents a hotbed of opportunities. Toothbrushes are particular targets. A second grader decided to use "little pieces of soap in the bristles" for a better cleaning job than she could obtain from mere toothpaste. For the eventuality that "you get an important phone call," a fifth grader added a cell phone to a toothbrush and hairbrush combination.

One fifth grader seriously suggested a "Drive-Thru Dentist." After the dentist finishes working on a patient in the car at a first window, "he pulls in towards the second window to pay."

A young inventor, whose basement flooded occasionally, invented an alarm comprising a battery, a buzzer, and two spring-loaded electrical contacts separated by an aspirin tablet. When water in the basement reaches the aspirin, it dissolves, the electrical circuit is completed, and the buzzer alerts the family that water has entered the basement.

Another audible alarm was incorporated in a timer that was packaged in a bookmark to allow a sixth grader, engrossed in a book, to know when to stop reading.

One fourth grader introduced screens instead of glass for side windows of cars. That would not only prevent sheets of paper from blowing out of the car, but the screen would also "prevent things from flying into the window."

A first grader, having difficulty locating the ends of his seatbelt in the dark, invented "The Light Up Seatbelt."

All of these ideas resulted from problems the kids identified. Some of us never knew we had them. But isn't it a comfort to know the next generation is working on their solutions?

Kid Inventors: Food

As I recently mentioned, I've been involved with the New York State Invention Convention program for students between kindergarten and eighth grade. We ask them to solve a problem in a new way. A number of our young participants understandably are involved with food and other substances that have or should have flavors and scents.

For example, a third grader believed that bug sprays used at picnics should be tasty and edible, while still being effective bug repellants. She suggested flavors like "cherry squirt, chocolate mist, and salsa spray."

A sixth grader also objected to an odor. He thought gasoline could be improved by adding "roses, cinnamon, raspberry, and fresh air" scents to the gas.

A fourth grader thought combining ketchup and mustard would be simpler than having to apply them separately to a hamburger. He called the mix, "Ketchard." And speaking of condiments, a fifth grader inserted ketchup into french fried potatoes to eliminate a separate step and help prevent a sticky mess. Alternatively, maybe the mess could be prevented with a sixth grader's ketchup placed in a toothpaste tube.

Another fourth grader occasionally visits restaurants at which "the food is too expensive to eat." She invented "Edible Sunglasses" as a back-up plan.

A sixth grader, who identified a similar problem, invented "Hamburger Earmuffs" for "people who want to eat something when they are going through the snow."

A fourth-grade television watcher decided to attach a pizza machine to her TV. That is sure to save time and effort for the hungry viewer.

One seventh grader ran out of milk for his cereal, so he invented evaporated milk-coated cereal and he called it "Calcio." Just add water and you've solved a common breakfast problem.

A fifth grader invented a jar that has a screw top and a screw bottom, allowing the young user to reach peanut butter from either end, rather than coat a knife handle when he attempts to remove it from a standard jar.

A third grader invented a modular freezer, placed in a shopping cart to transport ice cream and other frozen goods while shopping at a supermarket.

A young inventor was never sure how hot his soup was before burning his tongue, so he combined a thermometer, a digital display, and a soup spoon. On a similar note, a first grader conceived of a bowl that turns colors from red to orange to blue depending on the heat of its contents. A second grader with a baby sister permanently attached a thermometer to a baby bottle so the baby's parents could see how hot the milk gets in the microwave oven.

A second grader observed that "babies are getting into medicine." Her solution was a fingerprint sensor in the cap of the prescription vial to "make sure it is a grownup thumb" that accesses the pills.

One second grader invented a see-through toaster, so you can see how toast is doing and know when it's the perfect time for it to come out."

Since cubicle-shaped milk cartons do not fit in round cup holders in a car, a third grader created a beverage container with a cubicle top portion and a cylindrical bottom portion.

It's only a matter of time before some of these ideas find their way into your local supermarket. Just remember, kids thought of each of them before a multinational company claimed credit.

Inventors: Alarm Clocks and Sibling Eliminators

One of the problems that seems universal among children and regular people is waking up in the morning.

The Invention Convention receives a significant number of alarm clocks and wake up machines each year. One invention featured a progressively louder audio recording repeating, "get up, Get Up, ..., GET UP!" Another alarm clock featured selectable, customized messages at 15-second intervals. Another included a nagging voice. The gentlest alarm clock, however, included a mother's loving audio message to get the heck out of the bed.

Some alarm clock inventions reflected a violent tendency among the inventors. A gloved hand was described to emerge at a high rate of speed from an alarm clock to "punch you in the eye" or "smack you in the face," apparently striking the sleeper into consciousness. A variation directed a mechanical hand to tickle the sleeper awake.

If a punching, smacking, or tickling hand failed to work, a sixth grader thought he had just the solution: a machine that "splashes cold water... onto my face." In fact, a number of disclosures squirted or threw water — always cold — to accomplish the wake-up task. A sixth grader invented a "Runaway Alarm" that squirted water and, with the help of a motion sensor, quickly moved away from the waking person who attempted to shut it off.

A second grader created a very scary robot to forcibly "pull you out of bed."

With invention titles like, "Shaker-Waker," "The Lift, Turn, and Tip," "The Tumble Alarm," and "Rock-Awake," you can easily imagine the inventive processes to "shake and wake you up."

But an eighth grader compassionately stated one side of the bed was to be tipped "gently... at 3 m.p.h. so there are no broken bones."

A thoughtful second grader devised a machine that would pinch and punch, but also "show a 'hologram' of mice" to rouse his father in time to take the student to school.

A fourth grader focused sunlight into a sleeper's shut eyes, while a less subtle second grader used a trumpet to do the job. A fifth grader invented a robot that first "brushes your teeth, combs your hair, gets you dressed" before actually waking the sleeper.

An eighth grader combined electrical paddles and a timer to create "the ultimate alarm clock." The disclosure is titled, "Defibrillator Alarm Clock" and the inventor promised, "nothing worse will happen to you all day."

Another popular category that seems to get the creative juices flowing in a student inventor is his or her younger siblings. Many student inventors are frustrated by younger siblings messing up their stuff, talking incessantly, or merely being underfoot. These situations resulted in solutions that range from elaborate contraptions culminating in an overturned bucket of water, to a "Sister Alarm Trap," complete with surveillance camera. "Toothpaste Glue" should be effective in shutting up the little kid. And a magical "Sister Begone" spray is self-explanatory, if not entirely based on the laws of physics.

For a precise, effective and downright low-tech solution, what could be simpler than a second grader's mouth tape fashioned to "stay on my sister's mouth every weekend and all summer.

Laughing and Applauding

The 1970s was the decade of laugh tracks on sitcoms. I remember *The Cosby Show* and *All in the Family*. Every time a toilet flushed on those shows, the laughter would explode. Go figure.

A laugh track (or laughter track) is a separate soundtrack for a recorded comedy show containing the sound of audience laughter. In some productions, the laughter is a live audience response instead; in the U.S., where it was most used, the term usually implies artificial laughter, also known as canned laughter or fake laughter, made to be inserted into the show.

We can thank the American sound engineer Charles "Charley" Douglass for inventing the laugh track. Let's give him a round of canned applause.

The Douglass laugh track became a standard in mainstream television in the U.S., dominating most prime-time sitcoms from the late 1950s to the late 1970s. By the 1980s, the Douglass family was eventually out-rivalled by other sound engineers who created stereophonic laugh tracks different from the original analog track. Also, many single-camera sitcoms by this time started diverting from a laugh track altogether to create a more dramatic environment.

Douglass, unsatisfied with the sweetening process, built a two-and-a-half-foot high device that looked like a mix of an organ and a typewriter. Its keys, when connected to the laugh recordings, created a range of response for any joke, big or small. One key produced a woman's laugh, another a child's; a mix would create big laughs, a single would create a minor one. Douglass even went so far as to update his device every few years or so, mixing and matching different laughs, retiring old and introducing new, to keep up with audiences. This not only gave that communal experience to people at home, but also helped shape the structure and pacing of modern sitcoms.

It was a revelatory moment for TV, one that most artists despised.

The hillbilly comic Bob Burns was on a show one time and threw a few of his racy and off-color folksy farm stories into the show. The show was recorded live but the sound engineers couldn't record the jokes. However, they did record the enormous laughs and placed them appropriately in following shows that weren't very funny.

Live audiences could not be relied upon to laugh at the "correct" moments; other times, audiences would be deemed to have laughed too loudly or for too long.

Network research suggested that the laugh track was mandatory in order to brand a single-camera show as a comedy. The experiment to see if a comedy fared better with a laugh track was tested in 1965 when CBS showed its new single-camera sitcom Hogan's Heroes to test audiences in two versions: one with the laugh track, the other without. Partly due to the somewhat cerebral nature of the show's humor, the version without the laugh track failed while the version with laughter succeeded. The show was broadcast with the laugh track, and CBS utilized a laugh track for all comedies afterwards.

I learned most of this information from the Wikipedia site, which you can search under "laugh track."

Generally, laughs are now much less aggressive and more subdued; you no longer hear unbridled belly laughs or guffaws. It's "intelligent" laughter — more genteel, more sophisticated. And flushing toilets don't get the guffaws they used to, thank goodness.

Nowadays, I'm watching late night talk shows and I've noticed every time someone makes the slightest reference to a city or state or length of marriage, he or she gets a round of applause. That seems pretty easy to do. To liven up the crowd, I'm planning to drop a few city names at the next cocktail party I'm invited to.

Applause today is what laugh tracks were in the '70s.

Luddites Among Us

Have you noticed that certain people have an aversion to trying new things? Some people would rather do it the old, hard way, than the easier, modern way.

One group of people whom I haven't been able to figure out is men. I don't know about men in other countries, but men in the U.S. have a strange desire to ignore an invention that has been around in one form or another since at least the first half of the last century. I'm speaking, of course, about toilet paper holders.

I've been a guest in modern American homes occupied by husbands and wives who have the benefit of higher education and significant income. The t.p. holder in the guest bathroom is often empty, but a toilet paper roll is balanced on the holder or perched on the toilet tank lid. The toilet paper holders in those homes appear to be perfectly functional and, in fact, often quite attractive. But the man of the home refuses to fill it with a new roll when the old one runs out.

In many countries, such as India, parts of Russia, and rural areas of Arab countries, people don't use toilet paper at all. That helps explain why only 27,000 trees are cut down worldwide to make toilet paper every day. But as usual, I digress.

Now it's true toilet paper holders are a relatively new invention compared to toilet paper itself, which replaced tree leaves and moss about the time paper replaced papyrus; but even so, t.p. holders have been around longer than, say, automatic transmissions that change gear ratios as a vehicle moves, eliminating the need to shift gears manually.

Speaking of automatic transmissions, the first one was invented in 1921 by Alfred Horner Munro of Regina, Saskatchewan. It used compressed air, but the ferocious noise didn't make up for its inefficiency. The first modern automatic transmission using hydraulic fluid was developed in 1932 by two Brazilian engineers who sold it to General Motors. It was introduced in the 1940 Oldsmobile as the "Hydra-Matic" transmission.

Now that I think of it, even though automatic transmissions have been around for 75 years, some people still buy cars with standard transmissions, requiring two hands and two feet to operate the vehicle, instead of one hand and one foot. When I engage cruise control, which I do even before I leave my driveway, I don't even need a foot. I find a single finger is often adequate, freeing my other hand to express my displeasure with other drivers on the road or to hold a slice of pizza and, afterwards, to text about the experience. (Just kidding: pizza can be way too messy.)

So here we have another excellent invention that some of us shun. It's as if those people would prefer to be living in 1920, technology-wise. I wonder if the same folks who drive manual transmissions also unroll their own t.p.

Speaking of motor vehicles, the starter motor was originally called an electric starter and was invented in the U.S. by GM engineers Clyde Coleman and Charles Kettering in 1911. (Yes, the same Charles Kettering who co-invented Freon about 15 years later.) The self-starting ignition was first installed in Cadillacs. Pundits believed that would be the end of the "boys only" club of drivers, because up to that time, only strong men could work the hand crank connected to the crank shaft to start their Model T. By 1919, though, all

135

Model Ts had starter motors. Women began driving and that's all I'm going to say about that, dear.

You don't see many people cranking their car engines nowadays, but for some reason, shifting gears manually is still popular among macho men and macho women. The same people who wouldn't think of sacrificing their T.V. remote controls are happy to operate their cars like it's still 1908. Go figure.

Someone should conduct a study connecting transmissions with toilet paper holders. Maybe "connecting" isn't the appropriate word, but you get where I'm drifting. Heaven knows, doctoral theses have been written on less important subjects, like fatalities due to tripping over shoelaces, which is a topic I will explore in greater detail when the time is right.

Now I am quickly approaching the finale of this informative, meaty essay, the part I refer to as the dessert. And what better accompaniment to most any dessert than whipped cream? Master chefs are often purists. They like to start with basic ingredients to create whipped cream: heavy cream, sugar, and perhaps a couple of drops of vanilla. Then they go to town with a frozen whisk and frozen mixing bowl. But really, what a time-consuming chore.

The Internet lists a dozen ready-to-use toppings, frostings, icings, coverings, decorations, and mousses. Some are all natural, some are all artificial, and some are combinations of the above. Surely one of them tastes as good as the old-fashioned, handmade variety. The 400 Friendly's ice cream parlors that use aerosol cans invented 80 years ago, by the way, can't be all wrong.

That's just another example of people preferring old ways over new ones. I'm going to explore this topic in greater detail as soon as I replace my typewriter ribbon.

My Best Inventions

I'm a pretty modest guy. You don't hear me bragging about my abilities, my education, my physical attributes, or — Lord knows — my net worth. But I am proud of my creativity. And a good way to show how creative I am is to tell you about my inventions.

For starters, it was I who first came up with the delicious combination of peanut butter and honey on a sandwich. I was about 11 years old at the time. It was one of the only dishes I could prepare all by myself. At the time, it was a revolutionary concept, arrived at after adding honey to hundreds of breakfast cereals, condiments, and baked goods, including lasagna. The peanut butter and honey concoction succeeded way beyond my kitchen to the extent that now supermarkets display jars of honey right next to the peanut butter. That's not a coincidence, I think.

Now in Colorado, some people dribble honey on pizza crust when they've eaten the middle, tasty part of the pie. It's a great idea. You should try it. Boy, I wish I had thought of that one twenty years ago. I would be the Chef Boyardee of pizza parlors from Florida to Colorado.

When you're very, very hungry, you can also thank me for double Whoppers, which I invented more than 40 years ago. I asked the manager at my local Burger King if he could slip in an additional beef patty to my Whopper. He said he'd be happy to do it for me, but he would have to charge me 25¢. I thought of requesting honey, too, but discretion prevailed. Now, of course, you can find double Whoppers at every Burger King. It's on the menu. But I'm sorry to report the original 25¢ surcharge is history.

When I was a teenager, I invented a toaster that automatically buttered bread as it heated up. The owner of the toaster could insert a bar of butter into a square hole at the top of the toaster and the heat of the toaster would melt the butter into a pool. A miniature lawn sprinkler between the two slices of bread would spray the liquid butter as the bread toasted. Efficiency could be improved when an army division, for example, had to be fed breakfast. The mess sergeant might want to use an 8-, 12-, or 50-slice toaster, the slices being arranged like a fence around the butter sprinkler.

A bar of margarine could be substituted for the butter. See? I thought of everything. I even had a sales slogan for the contraption: "Toast tastes better buttered." The drawback with the invention was what I considered the minor inconvenience of removing rancid butter accumulating in the base of the toaster.

That was the end of my culinary inventions.

In fifth grade, at the advanced age of ten, I invented a three-stage rocket. Seriously. Frankly, I'm not sure that really counts, as I might have overheard the concept mentioned by Mr. Wonderkrumpf, my science teacher. Anyway, I was excited to mail my idea to NASA in 1958, but it was never officially acknowledged. I guess they were too busy at the time.

I often hear music but I just can't place the title or artist. In this age of Google, I am used to instant gratification when it comes to tracking down trivia and going to bed with a tune rattling around in my head was driving me crazy. It seemed clear that a program to identify music instantly would be just the thing. So a few years ago I thought of a computer program that could identify recorded music playing in a room.

But a patent search, which is a prudent thing to do with inventions, uncovered a patent that had already issued. In fact, the app it described now resides on many people's cell phones. It's called Shazam, a better trademark than I could have come up with. It's an excellent program and I highly recommend it. But once again, just like the three-stage rocket, I was a bit too late to become rich and famous.

Many years ago, a skunk was doing what skunks sometimes do right outside my window. That terrible odor woke me up three mornings in a row. After silently cursing the little critter, I noticed I was waking up in a comparatively pleasant way. My heart didn't beat quickly like when I was awakened by an alarm clock or even a clock radio, no matter how quietly it was set. So I used this knowledge to invent a smelly alarm clock. I could use pressurized canisters, I thought, that would spray scents into the bedroom like skunk odors or perfume or coffee or frying bacon.

Again, I performed a patent search and discovered someone else had patented the concept only a few months earlier. His purpose was to awaken blind and deaf sleepers with the sense of smell. That was a humanitarian thing to do, of course, but it signaled the end of the smelly alarm clock project for me.

I also thought of a digital grandfather's clock that would include a pendulum but would have a digital display instead of the conventional analogue face. The problem I couldn't overcome was manufacturing. It would cost more for me to make the clock than I could possibly sell it for. For a guy who doesn't even wear a wristwatch, I seem to think about improving time pieces more than you would expect.

The same expensive cost of materials situation occurred with an adapter I invented to make a better electrical connection for appliances to be plugged into worn outlets. As you insert a plug into my adapter, which I called the "Snug Plug," the prongs of the adapter spread against the outlet, resulting in a firm mechanical connection to the wall. But the Snug Plug was awfully expensive to produce. Really, who would want to pay $20 for a little electrical adapter that didn't appear to be worth more than 79¢?

It's obvious that inventing is not my calling. As a patent attorney, I am content merely to help protect other people's inventions, much like a midwife helps deliver other people's babies. Mothers and inventors both conceive — babies and inventions, respectively.

Although I am not particularly successful as an inventor, I am even less successful in getting pregnant.

Noteworthy Occasions

You can't help but notice that Robert Conrad likes to concoct themes for his *Weekend Radio* broadcasts, when he can. Most often, he develops a theme around a particular day that some or most of us celebrate. It wasn't awfully long ago, for example, that a few of us, apparently, celebrated Doctors' Day. The entire *Weekend Radio* broadcast was dedicated to doctors and their day. I can hardly wait to hear what Mr. Conrad has in store for us on or around next June 16th, National Mortician's Day.

Jan C. Snow seems to be on top of famous days, too. Her essays can be counted on to mesh nicely with Valentine's Day, Thanksgiving, Christmas, and the Fourth of July.

Not wanting to be a me-too essayist — or MTE, for those of you into TLAs or three letter acronyms — I'm going to be proactive. I'm not going to wait for the New Year to resolve to write essays in anticipation of holidays and anniversaries. And not just any old famous days, either. I mean, really, anyone can knock out an insightful or humorous piece about Washington's birthday, right? You don't need me to get the conversation going about cherry trees or Presidents' Day sales.

No, I'm going to focus on more obscure days. For example, I see that National Caramel Popcorn Day is April 6th, National Hot Pastrami Sandwich Day is January 14th, and National Cleavage Day, sponsored by the Wonderbra Company, is in the beginning of April, even though National Bra Day is November 1st. I suppose you can have one without the other. Oh, speaking of which, don't miss National Tube Top Day on October 8th.

In addition to Cinco de Mayo, May 5th is also National Hoagie Day, National Oyster Day, and National Chocolate Custard Day.

National Junk Food Day is July 21st, not to be confused with National Fast Food Day on April 15th or National Greasy Foods Day, which happens to be my birthday. Being a modest fellow, I won't tell you what day that is.

At first, I, like most people, thought August 26th, had only one cause to celebrate: National Cherry Popsicle Day; but I've since learned that it's also National Toilet Paper Day. Who knew? You would think that the Toilet Paper Day in August would be closer to Thomas Crapper Day, but that's celebrated on January 27th.

On November 8th, you can celebrate a day commemorating a fictitious person as well as a drink named for him: National Harvey Wallbanger Day. It's also the birthday of Montana's statehood, but most of us would think that pales in comparison to Harvey Wallbanger. Hey, here's an idea: on November 8th, let's all meet in Missoula for a drink.

And speaking of drinks, National Coffee Day is September 29th or May 16th, depending on whose calendar you use, not to be confused with National Cappuccino Day, November 8th, which happens to be the same day as Harvey Wallbanger's, if you were paying attention. National Irish Coffee Day is celebrated on January 25th. Turns out, National Coffee Day is celebrated on different days in Brazil, Costa Rica, Ireland, and Japan.

Not all national days revolve around food and drink. On September 9th you can celebrate Talk Like a Pirate Day or

142

Talk Like a Mad Scientist Day on July 27th or perhaps Chew the Fat Day on August 14th. Or, if you're a masochist, you can find a way to celebrate Talk to a Telemarketer Day on July 16th.

There's a National Kazoo Day, believe it or not, on January 28th, but try not to spread that around. Likewise for National Accordion Day on January 13th.

I wonder which supermarket cashier came up with Keep the Change Day on May 29th or which domestic engineer came up with No Housework Day on April 7th.

Right before the end of the year, on December 30th, you can celebrate National Bicarbonate of Soda Day, which you will welcome if you've been properly observing the previous 360 odd days of the year.

However exotic these national days may seem, I can hardly expect *Weekend Radio* to feature one. No, I'm leaning away from a Wonderbra Cleavage Day or any other Hallmark holiday. I'm looking for an important day, an ancient day. And I think I've found one: Tzom Gedalya, the day that commemorates the assassination of the Governor of the land of Israel, Gedalya ben Achikam. It happened while the famous Babylonian King Nebuchanezzar was on his throne. Which reminds me: I haven't found a National King Nebuchanezzar Day, but stay tuned; I'll keep looking.

Online Recipes

I own 21 cookbooks. Each is filled with gorgeous photographs of items that should result merely by following the printed instructions. Foods are baked or fried or grilled. I can see from the photos alone that the prepared fish and chicken and roasts are juicy, savory, flavorful, and delicious. The colorful photos are so well presented in such incredibly sharp detail, I can almost hear the sizzle and taste the food.

Some of the pages are resistant to liquid ingredients that might splatter onto them in the course of preparing the dishes. That's an excellent idea. People who wouldn't think of reading bedtime stories at the kitchen table routinely and foolishly move their cookbooks to the kitchen, the most dangerous room of the house. It's only cookbooks that are subjected to such hazardous conditions this way. I've never seen pages of a Shakespeare play stained with spaghetti sauce, have you?

Cookbooks often have an ethnic theme, like Turkish or Italian cuisine. Or the theme might be soups or stews or hamburgers. One sort of food or spice might be featured with a title like "A Hundred Ninety-Nine Ways to Delight Your Family with the Same Old Chicken" or "Unless You're a Vampire, Garlic is Your Friend."

I acquired some of my books at food shows and conventions at which the authors were present to sign their books. They can become collectors' items — the books, not the authors — especially if the authors die early with, say, a chicken bone in their throat. So I hold onto the books while checking obituary columns.

All of my cookbooks have one thing in common: they've never been used. They are in perfect condition. It's not that I dine at restaurants three times a day. In fact, I love to cook and bake. I find the activity therapeutic. For me, cooking   as opposed to washing dishes — relieves stress. I find the process, especially the consuming part, particularly fulfilling.

The reason I never use my beautiful cookbooks is the Internet. The Internet has completely replaced my need for printed cookbooks. All of the world's knowledge, past and present, is at my fingertips. I can find a recipe for any dish in seconds. I can find multiple recipes for the same dish. So many recipes appear, in fact, that sometimes it's hard to choose which one to use. In those cases, I'll read reviews by amateur chefs like me.

I've discovered an interesting phenomenon among chefs who rate recipes: they will bestow a number of stars for the recipe, often five stars, and then proceed to explain how they changed the recipe by adding, subtracting, or substituting ingredients. It's not unusual to see comments like, "This is an absolutely perfect recipe, but I used only half the salt," or "My whole family loved this dish, but I substituted milk for the heavy cream."

Recently after hearing that Maine has a glut of lobsters this year, I decided to bake lobster pot pie. I doubt I could have found that extravagant recipe in one of my cookbooks, even if I had decided to open one. Sure enough, I found a few recipes online and selected one that looked irresistible. It had favorable reviews, including one whose reviewer decided to substitute a chicken for the lobster.

145

(Okay, just a little culinary comedy there.) The fact is, as expected, the lobster pot pie is as wonderful as it sounds.

Here's another Internet recipe story. Last week I had an urge for the baked macaroni and cheese that Horn & Hardart's Automat used to sell. The Automat was a restaurant started in New York City and Philadelphia during the Great Depression. It's not around any longer. But it consisted of a large Art Deco room and banks of small windows along the walls. Each window had a prepared hot or cold dish of food. I would insert nickels into slots next to the food item I wanted and the door would spring open like in a Jetson's cartoon so I could extract my dish.

The food was wholesome and quite delicious, from Boston baked beans and chicken pot pie to rice pudding. The coffee was legendary, too, although I was too young to drink it at the time. Horn & Hardart whole roasted or ground coffee beans are available now — surprise! — on the Internet.

As for the baked macaroni and cheese, I did find the recipe on the Internet and, while browsing, discovered a book about the history of the Automat. It was written by two women, one of whom coincidentally has the name, Marianne Hardart. If you can't find that book at your bookstore, you can purchase that book on... oh, you know.

The macaroni and cheese recipe I found on the Internet was more elaborate than I expected, requiring more ingredients and more time than I had available. I printed it so I can try it some cold winter afternoon.

Until then, I'll reminisce about its flavor and the days that seven nickels could be inserted into the Automat window for a steaming hot casserole plate of the stuff.

Ordering in Advance

Recently, I visited a very nice Italian restaurant – you know, the type that has tablecloths – and I ordered from the menu. While waiting for the server to deliver my meal, it occurred to me that I could have saved time if I had called in or emailed my order in advance. With the right timing, I could arrive at the restaurant, be seated, and have my meal in front of me in seconds. I wouldn't even have to delay my meal by hearing the server's name.

If I could save an average of only 6 minutes per meal, that would be equivalent to 30 minutes per week, or 26 hours every year. You see where I'm going with this. Every three decades of restaurant visits would result in a savings of about a month. That's a lot of time waiting for your soup, you have to admit.

I have to confess this is not an entirely novel idea. Many take-out restaurants encourage customers to place orders online, so the food will be waiting for them when they arrive.

But if it works for take-out restaurants, why wouldn't it work for sit-down joints?

It's just a matter of time before all restaurants offer this service. Just remember where you heard it first. Boy, it's exhausting having to push society into the future single-handedly.

Pi Day

Aphysicist named Larry Shaw worked at San Francisco's Exploratorium and became enamored with pi. For those of you who may have slept through part of the seventh grade, the ratio of a circle's circumference to its diameter is a number called pi (p-i) or the Greek symbol π. If you know a circle's diameter, you can easily calculate its circumference. This information is sure to come in handy when you want to impress a mathematician at a party.

The number is irrational, like some mathematicians, in fact, so the decimal places never end and never repeat. Pi can't be represented as a ratio of integers, so don't even try it. Trust me. It's also a transcendental number because it can't be produced by a finite series of calculations.

The value of pi starts with 3.14. Remember that figure, 3.14, because I'll mention it later.

Dr. Shaw looks a bit like a mischievous Santa Claus with a perpetual smile, a full white beard, and a LOT of unkempt hair. You can see his photograph by googling him. He was so interested in the number pi, in fact, he created a special day to celebrate pi and called it Pi Day (or Pi Dī, if you happen to be visiting from Australia). Pi Day is a lot easier to enunciate than Circumference-to-Diameter-Ratio Day. Although Larry Shaw retired, the Exploratorium continues to host an annual celebration now at Pier 15 in San Francisco.

The first Pi Day was March 14, 1988. March 14th. 3/14. Get it? So far, so good. Coincidentally, March 14th also happens to be Albert Einstein's birthday, which meets my quota of trivia for this essay. You can find other people born on March 14th or, for that matter, on any day, including your birthday, by checking famousbirth-days.com. If you happen to be in Princeton, New Jersey on Einstein's birthday, feel free to enter the annual Einstein look-alike contest.

Now back to pi. Since 1988, more and more people have celebrated Pi Day and in 2009, the U.S. House of Representatives officially designated March 14th National Pi Day. The Admissions Department of M.I.T., the Massachusetts Institute of Technology, mails its decision letters to students so they are delivered on Pi Day. Oops, now I've done it: I've just exceeded my trivia quota.

If you divide 22 by 7 you get a reasonable approximation of pi. So someone decided to name 22/7, that is, July 22nd, Pi Approximation Day. That way, obsessed math students could celebrate two days each year.

People in San Francisco observe the day by dressing up in appropriate, usually gaudy clothing and flashy jewelry, marching around in a Pi Procession, eating all sorts of pies, of course, and conducting discussions, presentations, and demonstrations. One year, Albert Einstein in puppet form sang a rap about pi. Sometimes people toss pies and pizza dough at each other.

Some people recite pi to as many decimal places as they can remember, but none of the participants comes close to Akira Haraguchi, the world record-holder who recited more than 83,000 decimal places for pi. I have to admit that's pretty impressive to me, who can't even remember my cholesterol numbers.

This March 14th, 2015 is especially significant, because the first ten digits of pi are represented sequentially as the date and time: 3/14/15 at 9:26:53 a.m. (Or p.m. if you want to sleep in that Saturday.)

The history of pi is interesting, even if you aren't a mathematician. Egyptians were able to approximate it way back in the 26th century B.C. and mathematicians have improved on the accuracy ever since. Through the years, Archimedes, Isaac Newton, and a host of amateurs have taken a shot at calculating a better, more accurate value of pi. It wasn't until 1748 A.D. that Leonhard Euler used the Greek letter to represent pi. And about 150 years later, in 1897, the Indiana legislature, bless them, came close to passing a law declaring pi exactly equal to 3.2. But smarter heads prevailed.

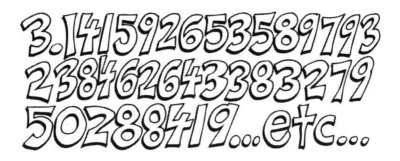

Starting in 1949, computers were enlisted to fight the battle of the precise value of pi and things really took off. The number of decimal places of pi started at 2,000 and reached 100,000 only 12 years later. They reached 100 million in 1987. A few web sites include the first million decimal places for pi. Here's an easy web site to remember to see all million numbers: www.EveAnders- son(with two s's).com/pi.

The 1990s witnessed computers displaying a billion, tens of billions, and even hundreds of billions of decimal places for pi. Recently home computers were used to calculate pi to 14 trillion decimal places, rivaling our national debt. What am I saying? Our national debt is trillions of dollars greater, now more than $17 trillion.

All of these lofty numbers make me dizzy. That's just one of the reasons I'll never aspire to the job of Secretary of the Treasury.

I think I'll take a nap right after I warm up an apple or blueberry... MUFFIN!

Redesigning Humans

At the risk of playing God, genetic researchers will have some excellent options in the future, in addition to preventing diseases like hemophilia, diabetes, color blindness, Alzheimer's, and everyone's favorite: cancer. In their spare time, those scientists might consider improving the physical aspects of human beings. To that end, I humbly propose adding a few items to the wish list for future geneticists.

For starters, I'd like to see a future generation of people who do not have ten toes. It might have been a good idea to have toes when we were swinging from trees, but nowadays, I don't see much use for them. We could save money and time if we didn't have to cut our toenails or, in some cases, paint them every few weeks. And what's the main body part that gets stubbed when you're walking down the hallway in the dark? Exactly!

I suppose if eliminating all toes sounds too drastic for sentimental reasons, we can limit the number of remaining toes to one toe per foot for a while and see if people would get used to that. Then, a century or two later, we can dispense with that toe and no one would miss it. Outside of a few pedicurists and podiatrists, who could have a problem with doing away with some or all of their toes?

And speaking of lower extremities, I've noticed a good number of people – young and old, drunk and sober – having balancing problems, all stemming from the fact that we only have two legs. You don't see cats and dogs and cockroaches tripping or falling over, no matter how much they drink, do you? Perhaps future versions of humans could have three legs instead of two. We'd be walking human tripods. We would all be more stable, and sock and shoe manufacturers would appreciate an additional 50% more income. While they're at it, and since we're doing away with toes, scientists might consider retractable wheels at the bottom of our three feet. The advantages are obvious.

I think an extra eye at the back of our head could come in handy when backing up or keeping track of snowboarders behind us on a ski mountain. Twisting one's head is both inefficient and sometimes dangerous. We could also engage in people-watching more freely and clandestinely.

We might also consider adding an ear to the top of our head, to provide an early warning system in case water balloons or drones or flying ducks are nearby.

Someone should do something about the human age limit. A lifespan of only one hundred or so years seems entirely too short to accomplish much, especially when we waste so much time at supermarket checkout counters and highways during rush hour. I think society will be able to deal with doubling or tripling our life expectancy. Of course, no one would want to have a 300-year-old body that looked like one, so we'd have to figure out a way to keep old people looking and feeling younger... a lot younger.

Overall, I'd like people to have improved senses. It would be helpful to have a sense of sight like an eagle and a sense of smell like a dog. Improved hearing could also be useful, especially for a few octagenarians I happen to know.

Here's another thought: let's make bones unbreakable.

Improving memory at least a hundred-fold would also come in handy for students, for people who play *Jeopardy!*

and for adults who have met tons of people at cocktail parties over the last two or three centuries.

Let's also hook up our brains to the Internet wirelessly, so we won't have to lug cell phones or laptops or whatever else 300-year-olds will be carrying in the future.

Stressful Computers

As I was deleting most of my email the other day, it occurred to me that I had previously read two-thirds of the jokes I received that day. I suppose you'll know when you're ready to check out for good when ALL of the jokes you receive are familiar. I mean, what else is there left to live for if not for new email jokes?

I can't remember an email joke as well as I can when a joke is told to me, face-to-face. Somebody should do a study. Maybe I ought to start reading my email jokes out loud.

I'll tell you, seriously, what ought to be studied: that's the effect that computers have had on our stress level. There seems to be nothing more frustrating than dealing with an uncooperative program. You knock yourself out trying to think of every possible cause for the darn computer not responding like it should and still it defies you. I can't tell you how often I've thought about throwing the machine out my window just to hear the satisfying crunch it will make when it hits the pavement. I think it will be worth the replacement value for that one second of retribution.

I can foresee anthropologists sometime in the future reporting on the fact that our life spans continued to increase, year by year, through the 18th and 19th centuries and halfway into the 20th century, all the way up to the time that computers were invented, at which point we started to die younger. Let's face it, how much anxiety occurred in the Stone Age when all you had to worry about was whether the sun would come up the next day and whether your spear would be waiting for you where you placed it the night before? And how many farmers died young in the 16th century concerned about whether their corn would grow? In the late 19th century, were people really nervous that their train wouldn't arrive because of a threatened air traffic controllers' strike?

Those guys had it easy, compared to your average office worker of today, coping with word processors run amok, spewing page after page of drivel, or spread sheets that don't stop spreading.

No, we've reached the ultimate stress factor, I think, with computers. It's just a matter of time before we use up every psychiatrist in our country dealing with our neuroses.

Hey, maybe there's an app for that.

Supercentenarians

It's not too difficult to live to 100. After all, in the world more than a third of a million people are that old right now. In fact, people who reach the age of 100 years or more are the fastest growing part of the population.

About 1 person in every 6,000 reaches their 100th birthday today. That may not seem like great odds, but it sure beats the lottery.

The United States has the most centenarians -- about 72,000. If the population of centenarians continues to increase at its current rate of expansion, a million people of 100 years of age or more will be in the U.S. by 2050.

In total numbers of centenarians, Japan is second to the U.S., with a current population of about 30,000. At its current rate of expansion, by 2050 Japan proportionally will have the most centenarians in the world.

Let's take a look at the really old population, the folks who live beyond 100. Only about one in 1,000 people who live to the age of 100 make it to 110. Those people are called supercentenarians.

The oldest person who ever lived, if you don't include biblical characters, is Jeanne Louise Calment [ʒan lwiz kalmã] who died in 1997 at the age of 122½ years. We don't even have a word for people that old.

Jeanne outlived both her daughter and her grandson. Some of her close family members also lived an above-average lifespan: her brother lived to the age of 97, her father to 93, and her mother to 86.

In 1896, at the age of 21, she married what we call her double second cousin, Fernand Nicolas Calment. Their paternal grandfathers were brothers, and their paternal grandmothers were sisters. Anyway, they were married 46 years and her husband died at the age of 73, some 55 years before she did, of cherry poisoning. Guess we all have to go from something, eventually.

Jeanne's husband was wealthy, so she could employ servants and never had to work. She took care of her skin with olive oil and a puff of powder. She led a leisurely lifestyle in high society, pursuing hobbies such as fencing, cycling, tennis, swimming, roller-skating, playing the piano, and making music with friends. I envy her having so much time for hobbies. Actually, I envy her having so much time for everything.

She had one daughter who died of pleurisy on her 36th birthday.

In 1965, aged 90 and with no heirs left, Jeanne signed a life estate contract on her apartment, selling the property in exchange for a right of occupancy until her death. The fellow who bought her place probably thought she'd die any day now and he'd be able to occupy the apartment. But he died in 1995, by which time Jeanne had received more than double the apartment's value from him. And his family had to continue making payments. Jeanne said, "in life, one sometimes makes bad deals." How's *that* for an understatement?

A study of 20 people worldwide who reached at least 115 years of age, stated that the lives of these people differed widely. They had just a few common traits: most of them were female (only two were male), most smoked little or not at all, and they had never been obese. Although they aged slowly, all became very frail and their physical fitness declined markedly, especially after age 105. Surprise! In their final years, they required wheelchairs and were nearly blind and deaf.

A good number of celebrities lived to 100 and you can find them on Wikipedia if you search for "List of Centenarians." A few that come to mind are: Olivia De Havilland, Bob Hope, Queen Elizabeth (the Queen Mother), George Burns, Kirk Douglas, and David Rockefeller.

A doctor in England, Alex Zhavoronkov, believes that life expectancy is now much greater than we believe. He is 37 years old and takes 100 different drugs and supplements each day, exercises regularly, goes for frequent checkups, and monitors his own blood biochemistry and cell counts. He also claims to have suppressed cravings for marriage, children, and material assets to concentrate on anti-ageing research. He says, "I think that even people past their 70s, who are in good health, have a fighting chance to live past 150." For some reason, I really like Dr. Z and I haven't even met him.

I began to wonder about the occupations or professions that had the best chance of living a long time. You know, it's never too late to change occupations.

I found way too many contradictory articles on the Internet and ended up being pretty confused. There's only one thing that seemed to be constant among professions: women live longer than men. I know I just said it's never too late to change, but if I were to become a woman, I'd have to invest in a whole new wardrobe and maybe do something about my bald head.

Tie Racks & Mezuzahs

As I unpacked what seemed like thousands of moving boxes on my recent relocation to Colorado, I was delighted to discover, amidst a morass of tangled neckties, a tie rack that has been with me all my adult life. The tie rack measures 16" and has 24 metal prongs that collapse against each other, like falling dominoes, for storage. When the prongs are extended outwardly and parallel to each other, you can place a necktie over each one, so all of your ties can be displayed neatly.

This tie rack isn't produced anymore, but you might find one for sale on eBay. It's a good idea to be prepared, in case you suddenly decide to become a presidential candidate and you need neckties. The trademark on the tie rack I just found is KOVAX (K-O-V-A-X). The tie rack was patented in the late 1940s, about the time I was born.

The reason I know so much about this product is because my maternal grandfather — Louis Kovacs, spelled with a "cs" not an "x" — was the tie rack inventor. He manufactured them for many years.

In 1972 I asked him about the history of the necktie, thinking who better would know its origin.

He said, in his most kindly, grandfatherly voice, "How the heck should I know, Mark? Just Google it."

No, he didn't refer to Google in 1972, decades before the Internet. But he did tell me he had no idea of the necktie's origin. He merely wanted to help people organize them. Trying to bunch slippery, silk ties on a clothes hanger can result in a clump of ties, like cooked spaghetti, deposited on the closet floor.

Grandpa Louie was the first inventor I ever met. I've since discovered many of them are not as acerbic. I suppose it's not too much of a stretch to think the seed of my desire to become a patent attorney could have been sewn by him and his KOVAX tie racks.

Not long after I uncovered my tie rack during the move, I opened another box to discover a mezuzah. A mezuzah, as you may recall from your bar mitzvah, is a generally rectangular case about the size of two cigarettes, side by side, made of wood, metal, or ceramic. Inside this case is a short Hebrew prayer printed on a miniature scroll of rolled-up parchment.

The prayer is copied from the Old Testament — from Deuteronomy 6:9 to be exact — exhorting Jews to write some commandments "upon the doorposts of thy house and upon thy gates."

The biblical ten plagues, we all know, culminated in the Angel of Death smiting Egyptian firstborn sons. But the Israelites, knowing what was coming, smeared sacrificial lambs' blood on their doorposts so the Angel of Death would pass over the Jewish homes and concentrate on the Egyptians'. Hence the name of the holiday — Passover — which is celebrated every year and commemorates the end of Jews as slaves in Egypt.

As time went on, it became clear that dried lambs' blood represented a health hazard. Besides, it was becoming more difficult to obtain sacrificial lambs' blood. There just weren't enough lambs to go around. Also, over time, since the Angel of Death hadn't made another appearance, the urgency for animal blood protection subsided.

But traditions and rituals die hard, and so to this day, you can find Jewish homes and Florida condos with a mezuzah nailed to the doorpost of their front door. More observant Jews also place mezuzahs on interior door frames in an abundance of caution, I guess. We want to advise the Angel of Death of the nationality or religion of the occupants, in case he missed the mezuzah at the front door or entered the dwelling, as angels sometimes do, by some other means.

If I hadn't unpacked my tie rack and my mezuzah on the same day, I might not have made the connection. But the fact is, as a symbol of inventiveness and legacy, Grandpa Louie's tie rack means more to me than my mezuzah.

I was tempted to nail the tie rack itself to my front doorpost, but it occurred to me that would be both silly and potentially sacrilegious.

So now I'm looking for an artist who can miniaturize the tie rack and hollow it out. I can then roll up a printed prayer or at least a clever essay in the tie rack before fastening it to my house. Thanks for the tie rack, Grandpa.

Too Much of Everything

I thought I'd buy a relatively inexpensive sports car. The one I had in mind is an Dodge Charger SRT Hellcat with a V8 engine and 707 horsepower. It can reach 204 miles per hour. But the speed limit on the interstate in my neighborhood is only 65. I just hate to waste the 139 extra miles per hour that car is capable of.

My existing Ford sedan has room for five people, but I'm usually driving it alone or with only my wife. That seems like a waste of three or four seats most of the time.

Do you see where I'm going with this? I think I simply have too many resources for my ability to use them. I live at a time of excess that goes beyond my ability to use even a few of my options.

Here's another example:

I contemplated buying a stereo system for my daughter's apartment. The speakers are so powerful, they can shatter her living room windows. But the home owner's association limits her volume and the time of night she can listen to music.

Recently, I visited an all-you-can-eat buffet at a casino a few miles away. The prime rib was absolutely huge. Frankly, I've never seen a chunk of meat that big that wasn't on a live bison. It was placed next to an impressive mountain of crab legs and that, in turn, was positioned just a little north of a mound of pasta. Even if I could have approached the carving station ten times, I couldn't have made a dent in the slab of beef. Ditto for the crab legs and pasta. As it turned out, I refilled my plate only five times before I developed a colossal stomach ache. What a disappointment.

I live in a house with so many rooms, some of them don't get visited more than once a month, and that's only to remove the accumulated dust. I use only one bed and one bedroom. I don't even know how many extra bedrooms are in my house.

I have a gas range that is capable of a high setting. But I was told that using that setting results in burning my pots and pans and the food in them. So, I have to limit the setting to medium, at most, so my wife herself doesn't overheat, too.

I thought I wanted to purchase the complete works of Mozart on CDs. The collection ran to 200 CDs, representing months of listening for a mere $368. And what a deal... if I included the complete works of Beethoven (86 discs), Chopin (17 discs), and Bach (142 discs), a total of 445 CDs, I could get them all for under $1,000. Between reading books and album liners about the composers and performers, I figured I could listen to one CD per night for a year and still have about three months of music to spare.

Speaking of entertainment centers, I can now access hundreds and hundreds of cable T.V. channels. But how many channels do I regularly see? About three of them.

My computer has a memory so large, I'd have to store 250,000 of these essays before I fill it up. Even if I could knock out one every hour, day and night, that would take me about 29 years if I limit myself to 30-minute lunches. As charming and interesting as I am, I still believe my audience wouldn't have the patience to hear me expound on 250,000 more subjects. I mean, how trivial can I possibly get?

My computer, along with the Dodge Charger I won't buy and the stereo system my daughter won't get and the gas range that I'm not permitted to use and the complete works of a handful of classical composers, is simply too big for me.I have more than enough of almost everything I can think of (except money, of course), but there's one thing I don't have and can't create. That's time. I could certainly use more of that.

Vanity Plates and Domain Names

Domain names, as you probably know, are the Internet letters or words that identify web sites. Domain names like Amazon, Google, Facebook, YouTube, and eBay are now household words in most American houses. Rumor has it that every single word in the English dictionary and every short combination of letters are already domain names.

I've tried about 9,000 so far, but I've been able to find only one word that is available as a domain name: phthisic.com. That's spelled p-h-t-h-i-s-i-c, for all of you Scrabble players. Phthisic has an archaic meaning: a wasting illness of the lungs. I just located that definition on the Internet, which reminds me... I was talking about Internet domain names, wasn't I?

At this point, in addition to single words and combinations of letters, many slogans, expressions, contractions, abbreviations, slang terms and made-up words are also registered as domain names. In fact, with billions and billions of web pages on the Internet, it's almost as difficult to choose a domain name that isn't already taken as it is to name a celebrity who's never been in rehab.

This subject reminds me of pre-Internet days when motor vehicle departments started to allow people to obtain their own personalized or so-called "vanity" license plates, as long as they were not obscene or slanderous. Too bad the Internet doesn't have the same policy, but that's a topic for a future essay.

California alone has over one million vehicles with vanity plates. That's more cars than there are people who live in Montana. In Virginia, one out of six drivers has a vanity plate. That may be because the registration fee is lowest there: $10.

The challenge is to make a meaningful statement within the length of a license plate that can accommodate only a handful of characters.

Squishing a message into a few letters on a license plate turned out to be good practice for people who email or text each other nowadays. There's no need to spell out "you are great," for example, when that expression can be conveyed in only four letters and a number: the characters "u r gr 8." An even shorter texted message could be "you are late," but the letter "L" with the number "8" could be misinterpreted to mean "you are 18," which would have a flattering effect for recipients above the voting age. But let's face it: how many seniors are texting, anyway?

Now back to motor vehicles. You can clearly see how vanity license plates led inevitably to efficient texting on the Internet. To put it another way, modern texting could not have occurred until cars and license plates were invented. That's just one more thing we have to thank Henry Ford for. Don't you love it when random technical and social cause and effects come together? Well, now I'll go back to working on my unified field theory.

STRANGE
OBSERVATIONS

A Connoisseur of Prescription Vials

O ver the years, I've had my share of pains, ailments, and diseases. I won't bother going into a litany of them, but suffice it to say only a few of my organs have escaped the ravages of living well in America until late middle age.

From my scalp to my toes, including my bones, blood, muscles, fat, and hair, each precious living piece of me has come under the care of a medical specialist or two over the years. I've been prodded, poked, pierced, and x-rayed more times than the Shroud of Turin.

The upshot of all of my tests has ranged from stern words of warning to friendly advice regarding exercise and diet. But most of all, the result of so many visits to physicians has resulted in remedies in the form of prescription drugs. I have accumulated dozens and dozens of vials of (mostly) expensive medications. With only a few exceptions, the vials are now empty. But through some perverse sense of accomplishment, I find it impossible to discard an empty vial. Some are small, some are large, some are jumbo. They are cylindrical, pyramidal, or square. Some held liquids, but most held pills, tablets, and capsules. Like family photographs, each one has a history behind it and I enjoy reliving the circumstances that prompted each prescription.

Over the years, I've purchased ever-larger cabinets to hold my collection of vials. Originally, I sorted them by function – pain relievers, antibiotics, vitamins, anti-inflammatories, controlled substances, statins, depressants,

171

stimulants, and anabolic steroids. But the collection got bigger and bigger and some of the categories overlapped.

So now I alphabetize them by brand names, not generic names, which can be ridiculously long and unpronounceable. From Abilify to Zytiga, I've got an impressive collection. Of course, my collection is thin in certain areas – like treatments for schizophrenia – and non-existent in others – like female fertility drugs – but all in all I have a collection I'm proud of. That's not to say it can't be improved, and I'm about 3 million vials short of completion. But in the next few decades, I plan to fill in at least some of the gaps.

I've got a good number of duplicates, as you would imagine, due to chronic conditions, so I'm now intent on trading vials with people who would appreciate my more esoteric empty vials. I, in turn, would be happy to acquire the vials that contained less common prescriptions, especially if the shapes of those vials were unique.

But alas, there just aren't as many prescription vial collectors as there are of fine art, coins, stamps, records, jewelry, baseball cards, books, magazines, barbed wire, or tea pots. Sadly, I've come to the conclusion that I may be the only one. In which case, I could well have the biggest collection of vials in existence.

There may be a prescription for patients with an irrational desire to collect empty prescription vials. If there is, I know exactly where I'll store that vial.

America, the Soap Opera

L ately, I've become as addicted to watching TV broadcast network news as my grandmother was to her TV soaps.

My grandmother followed three or four soap operas — she called them her "stories" — every weekday afternoon since about 1963. You couldn't interrupt her two-hour obsession from 2:00 p.m. to 4:00. She never made appointments that impinged on that sacred time slot and she didn't answer the phone, even for her half-dozen, darling grandchildren, I being the first born and most darling of them all.

For those of you who don't watch or even own a TV now, a soap opera is a serial melodrama with a number of plots and subplots dealing with the emotional lives of actors who recur from story to story until they demand a higher salary, at which point their character dies off from some mysterious disease or gets pregnant and leaves town. The term "soap opera" comes from the fact that the shows were broadcast in the afternoons, directed mostly towards housewives, and the sponsors were mostly laundry and hand soap manufacturers.

I can see similarities in the present broadcasting approach of TV news shows. For starters, the announcer's voice still imperiously begins the broadcast over some theme music, just the way grandma's stories began. The same network news anchors and the same reporters appear every evening at 6:30, their appointed time on all three respective major networks.

And some of the same story strands linger from night to night. For example, even excluding weeks or months leading up to an election, I can follow the progress of murder trials, political scandals, natural catastrophes, and threats of war as they slowly develop over many weekdays. Where I live in south Florida, during the hurricane season I am particularly sensitized to ongoing stories of weather disturbances or depressions in the Atlantic Ocean that can lead to tropical storms and beyond.

One difference between grandma's soaps and my news shows is the sponsors. My grandmother was subjected to ads for hand soaps, detergents, and shampoos, whereas I am bombarded only with repetitive reminders to ask my doctor about medications for what I had thought were obscure medical conditions but which I now know are much, much more prevalent. In fact, the commercials are so convincing, I'm pretty convinced I have contracted all of the ailments the medications can cure.

Another difference between grandma's stories and the nightly news is, usually, an upbeat, two-minute human interest story at the end of the half-hour barrage of bad news. The soaps, however, ended with what appeared to be no way out for the characters — or at least for the nice guys. That way, my grandmother and her friends were sure to tune in the next day to find out how the issues du jour would resolve.

Perhaps the major difference between my grandmother's viewing habits and mine is the remote control. I can now follow news broadcasts on four or five networks at the same time, but grandma was stuck watching her stories serially, unless she extricated herself from her couch to change channels by turning her TV dial. TV producers used to entreat her, "Don't touch that dial," when she had a dial to touch. That command just doesn't make sense nowadays.

You can appreciate how escalating terrorism and counter-terrorism retaliation tactics must be carried out by noticing the war between TV networks and interactive couch potatoes like me. For us, it's similar to a chess game in which the chess clock is replaced by the viewer's bladder.

The networks realized that people with remotes could switch among the channels easily to avoid commercials, so they all synchronized their programs to play commercials at the same time. I find it interesting, for example, to locate two channels showing a commercial for the same rheumatoid arthritis medication a few seconds apart. I can switch back and forth between the two channels, since I have nothing else to do but flex my joints to check for arthritis while I wait the 4½ minutes between news briefs — I mean stories.

It didn't take long for some of my fellow viewers and me to start using video tape recorders or, now, DVRs to record the programs so we could skip the commercials and watch entire 30-minute programs in 16 minutes.

What the networks have in store for us next is anyone's guess. If you are as anxious to find out as I am, don't touch that dial.

Amazing Human Talent

D o you know how long it takes the world champion to solve Rubik's Cube? When Ideal Toy Company introduced it in 1980, the company said there were more than three billion combinations, but just one solution. Actually, the number of combinations for a 3x3x3 Rubik's Cube is a staggering 43 quintillion — that's 43 billion billion or 1 with 18 zeroes after it. I guess the company didn't want to scare away its customers. A small number like three billion is much friendlier, don't you think? The company knew what it was doing: Rubik's cube is considered to be the world's best-selling toy.

But the number 43 quintillion is small potatoes compared to the number of possible games that can be played on a chess board. That number, for games of up to 40 moves, is greater than a quintillion quintillion, most of which, I would guess, Bobby Fisher played, or at least thought about playing.

The record holder for a particular type of simultaneous chess game is Marc Lang of Günzburg, Germany, who played 46 games simultaneously in 2011. All of his opponents had chess boards in front of them, but he played blindfolded, so he couldn't see the boards. He lost two of those games, which indicates to me that he wasn't that hot.

But back to the Rubik's Cube record holder. Feliks Zemdegs, the Australian 16-year-old world champion, is able to eliminate the 43 quintillion combinations of the cube that don't work to come up with the solution in fewer than six seconds. You can see him do it on YouTube, and you'll be impressed with his physical dexterity, too. Frankly, it takes me more than six seconds to arrange two blue tiles next to each other.

Feliks and the chess master, Marc Lang, are only two of the most talented people in the world. Consider people with savant syndrome.

Daniel Tammet memorized the value of π to more than 22,000 places, which is peanuts compared to the 100,000 digits that Akira Haraguchi is reputed to recite. But let's put things in perspective. The value π has been calculated by computers to trillions of places, so Haraguchi-san has a long way to go.

Kim Peak, the role model for the character Raymond Babbitt, played by Dustin Hoffman in the movie, Rain Man, was considered a megasavant. He could read two pages of a book at the same time, his right eye reading one of the pages and his left eye reading the other. Of course, he memorized every word of the 12,000 books he had read. But you know, he wasn't able to button his shirt. Not to brag, but I can button most of my shirts without even looking. So *there*, Kim.

Some savants can multiply really big numbers in their head. There's even a competition for them called the Mental Calculation World Cup. A few years ago, Marc Jornet Sanz from Spain multiplied two 8-digit numbers in his head in about 45 seconds. Just try to multiply, say, 84,378,211 by 77,490,528 in your head. Go ahead. I'll wait. I think of Señor Sanz every time I try to balance my checkbook.

Some savants can tell you the day of the week for any date in history from the years 1600 to 2100. On the other hand, I can't remember yesterday's date. Sometimes I don't even recall what month we're in. I do know that I was born on a Monday, but no one seems to care.

Other savants can determine the number of matches that fall on a floor, merely by glancing at them. If you meet one of these savants in a bar, don't bet against him.

Of course, people don't have to be savants to be extremely talented. A long time ago, mainframe computers had toggle switches and little lights above them. As the computer programs ran, you could see the 32 lights change rapidly from on to off or vice versa. Each movement of the lights represented lines of programming code, sometimes called assembly language or machine language. Of course, to most of us, those lights just looked like a pretty display, indicating that the computer was thinking.

I worked with a fellow at a computer manufacturing company back then, a very smart guy. How smart? At one point, I actually thought he might have come from outer space. He could set the computer processor to step through the statements of a program very slowly, command by command.

And here's the amazing part: he could actually "read" the blinking lights as the computer executed the program, step by step. When my co-worker came across a suspicious statement, he stopped the computer and corrected the statement in machine language. It was like watching Mr. Spock on Star Trek communicate directly with the computer, or like watching Dr. McCoy manipulating his high-pitched, reverberating, medical tricorder scanner.

Dr. Arthur B. Lintgen was so attuned to LP records, his fingertips could actually feel their way over the grooves of a vinyl record and he could tell what musical piece was recorded on it. Why buy an expensive turntable if you can hear the music without annoying your neighbors? Don't you wish you had a neighbor like Dr. Lintgen on Saturday nights?

Nowadays, many printed circuit boards for computers have layers of flat boards placed on top of each other. Imagine running a wire from a location on one of the boards to a location on another board. Now imagine doing it for 10,000 locations on one board to that many locations on another one. Now think of stacking and laminating 30 boards on top of each other and designing them so the wires don't cross each other. Only a handful of designers in the world can manage that feat. What a headache they must have every night.

Speaking of headaches, I started to think about musical composers who have done so much to relieve stress and headaches. Johann Sebastian Bach was prolific — and I'm not referring only to his 20 children here — I mean prolific as a composer. It would take a lifetime merely to copy every note he wrote onto sheet music paper. Imagine how much he could have composed if he had had an Apple computer and an outlet to plug it into.

Wolfgang Amadeus Mozart was a musical genius whose works are still played more than two centuries after he wrote them. He composed 41 symphonies, 27 piano concertos, 5 violin concertos, 36 violin sonatas, 4 horn concertos, cello, trumpet, clarinet, flute, bassoon, and oboe concertos and a host of string duos, trios, quartets, and quintets, and a passel of operas, masses, serenades, divertimentos, and marches. I'm out of breath just mentioning them all. Unfortunately for all of us, he died young. It's sobering for me to think that, when Mozart was my age, he was dead almost 30 years.

Humanity should be grateful for the incredible talent of super human people who have enriched our lives with acts of brilliance. Speaking of which, this essay has inspired me to take another crack at balancing my checkbook.

A Mountain for Everyone

Colorado has more mountains higher than 14,000 feet than any other state. The latest statistics — and they change every once in a while, depending on earthquakes, snowfall, moose droppings, or who knows what — the latest statistics indicate we have 54 peaks at least 14,000 feet high. On the other hand, the state of Colorado is only 22nd in population rank. That means every Colorado resident can have his own mountain, or almost.

So, I decided to choose my very own mountain peak based on height, location, and name, the name being important for only a short time, since I'm planning to rename my mountain "Mount Markie" as soon as I register it. I'm thinking the registration process should be straightforward with a minimal fee. I'm not sure where to do this, so I'll start at my local Department of Motor Vehicles. Those folks were right friendly when I exchanged my Florida Manatee license plates for the Colorado Rocky Mountain plates.   We have seven mountain ranges with high peaks. You can put away your pencils, because I won't give you a test on this. To start, we have the Elk Mountains, the Sawatch Range, the Tenmile Range, and the San Juan Mountains. The most exotic mountain range is the Sangre de Cristo and the most unfortunately-named range is the Mosquito Range. Last but not least — maybe because the explorers ran out of inspiring names — is the Front Range. Ironically, it's the Front Range that includes maybe the only mountain you may have heard of: Pikes Peak.

The highest mountain peak in Colorado is called Mt. Elbert. It's only 12 feet higher than Mt. Massive, which actually has five peaks higher than 14,000 feet at its various corners.

Just one foot under Mt. Massive is Mt. Harvard, coming in as the third highest mountain peak in Colorado. Harvard isn't used to being ranked third in anything, but that's the way the crimson cookie crumbles. At least it beats out Mt. Princeton, coming in at number 18. And that, in turn, is a whole foot higher than Mt. Yale, ranking as the 21st highest mountain.

In addition to Mt. Elbert and Pikes Peak, other peaks are named after people. We have Mounts Lincoln, Long, Antero, Evans, Wilson, Cameron, Sneffels, Lindsey, and Sherman. So, there's precedent for a Mt. Markie, you'll be happy to know.

You would think I might want to claim Mt. Elbert as my own, since it's the highest peak in Colorado. But there is sure to be a lot of competition for it. Same for Pikes Peak, since it's got that wonderful cog railway, "I made it to the top" bumper stickers, and all.

Sunlight Peak is a good possibility, but at night it's as dark as the rest of the mountains. So, it has a shadow of false advertising over its cap.

And Maroon Peak? Well, that sounds way too ominous and isolating.

Uncompahgre Peak might be ripe for a takeover, since so few people can pronounce it and fewer can spell it. I doubt I'd meet with many objections to renaming it Mt. Markie.

But head and shoulders above the other mountains for me is the one situated in the Tenmile Range. In fact, it's the only fourteener in that range. It's called Quandary Peak, tying with Castle Peak for 12th place.

Now all I have to do is find the Tenmile Range and Quandary Peak, which is no small task for a recent Floridian. It can be a... well, a quandary for me.

Back to Basics: Roman Numerals

A m I the only one who's pretty darn tired of those Arabic numerals we're all stuck with? I'm not saying they don't work, or that the person who invented the zero wasn't a genius. In fact, I think someone should award a Nobel Prize in mathematics posthumously, if we ever discover his or her name. Why not? You have to be dead for 10 years before you get a postage stamp issued in your honor. On second thought, a big zero on a postage stamp might be confusing, so forget the postage stamp idea. But the posthumous Nobel Prize is still a possibility. And think how much that would be worth now, with compound interest.

By the way, Arabs did not invent Arabic numerals. A person in India, reputedly a Hindu, did. Although how anyone knows his religion is beyond me. It happened around 500 A.D. How's that for trivia? The rest of the civilized world didn't adopt Arabic numerals for about 700 years. Some ideas just take longer to accept than others. Just ask Italo Marchiony, who may have invented the ice cream cone. Oh, bad example. Anyway, that's an essay for another time.

Well, let's get back to the Arabic numerals themselves. Sure, we can express size, distance, dates, and quantities conveniently. Sure, we can add, subtract, multiply, and the other thing I forgot. But where is the beauty, the elegance? Can numbers like 1 and 4 and 7 really rise to the aesthetic level of, say, MMDCXIV?

Obviously, I'm not alone in preferring Roman numerals for some things. That helps explain why the movie Rocky IV was popular, I think. More trivia: Sylvester

Stallone is an Italian American, as you probably know from his 1970 movie, *The Italian Stallion.*

How about athletic events? Who could possibly want to see Super Bowl XLVI referred to any other way?

For all you analog people out there, how convenient is it to have Roman numerals on your wristwatch? Or does anyone still have a wristwatch now that cell phones have taken over the planet?

Speaking of arithmetic operations, why can't we use Roman numerals to balance our checkbook? It's really very simple. Let me show you.

Let's say you have MLXII dollars in your checking account and you write a check for XII dollars to the IRS. MLXII minus XII equals ML. Simple, right?

"Ahh," you say. "But what if — now that the IRS is paid off — I want to write a check for, say, LIV dollars to donate to my public radio station? How do I subtract LIV from ML?"

"Just like with Arabic numerals," I say, smugly but patiently. You have to borrow an I from the sixth to last column, leaving DCCCCLLLLXXXXX or DCCCCLLLLXXXXVIIIII, if you're thinking ahead like Julius Caesar should have before he bumped into Brutus who was enjoying a pizza one day.

Now simply remove LIV, digit by digit, from that awfully long expression equivalent to ML, and what do you get? Let's see, VIIIII minus X, borrow from the closest D, move one of the Cs to the right column, make change of XXXXX. Of course, X minus IV equals VI, and the answer just falls out: MCMILVI. Easy as rigatoni. What could be simpler?

Honestly, with a bit of training, we can go back to basics, back to the good old days, just like the last 1600 years never happened.

Bobs Galore

As every precocious eight-year-old undoubtedly knows, a palindrome is a word or sentence that reads the same forward as it does backward. Among the many palindromes for nouns, like Mom and Dad, lurk some proper names: Anna, Eve, Hannah, and Otto, for example. The one I'd like to discuss now is *Bob*.

You know, we've had five Jameses, four Williams, and even a Barack, but there has never been a U.S. president named Bob. Now Scotland had King Robert the Bruce in the early 14th century, about the time the fork was invented, but that's an essay for another time.

Jon Bois, the Kentucky sports writer who spells his name B O I S, recently made an interesting observation. It appeared on SB — as in "sports blog" Nation.com: "Across the histories of Major League Baseball," he wrote, "the NFL, the NBA, the NHL, and NCAA football and basketball, there have been a total of 1,884 athletes who primarily went by the name Bob. Not Robert, or Bobby, but Bob." What Jon Bois found puzzling is that today there are precious few professional sports figures named Bob.

But the name, Bob, comes up in many other places.

Lake Bob, for instance, is located just outside of Baker City, Oregon.

In Africa, an entire country is called Zimbabwe, get it?

We don't have Linda-heads or Donald-heads, do we? But we sure have a huge variety of spring-necked bobble heads.

186

Socks named after Bobs are called bobby socks. And some hair pins are known as bobby pins. The Bob haircut comes and goes as a popular hairstyle for women.

We also have the plumb bob, shishkabob, the fishing bobber, apple bobbing, a carnivorous bobcat, a bobsled, a bobtail, and a bobstay for holding a ship's bowsprit down — something you might wish to keep in mind if you chance upon one of those untamable bowsprits.

We also have a sewing machine bobbin, of course, instructions to football players and boxers to bob and weave, the Bobbsey Twins series of books, and the North American bobolink blackbird, or Dolichonyx oryzivorus, for you ornithologists.

Bob and wheel is a type of alternative music rhyming pattern not too different from what you might see in a book of Ogden Nash poems.

But back to Bobs.

Bob's gym, Bob's Famous Roller Coaster in Chicago's Riverview Park, Bob's discount furniture, Bob's skateboarding tricks website, and the chain of Bob's stores that sell clothing and footwear — not necessarily made by Bobs — are just a few establishments that use Bob as a business name.

Have you been in a Bob's Steak & Chop House somewhere in the western states or in Australia, or the K-Bob Steakhouse in Albuquerque, or Billy Bob's Texas in Ft. Worth, reputed to be the world's largest honky-tonk? When you get there, say "howdy" to a Bob for me.

Bob Evans restaurants are not to be confused with Bob's Big Boy Restaurant, which — As delicious as they sound, Barbecue Bob and the Spareribs serves up not food, but country songs. Hurricane Bob struck the northeast coast in 1991, but I don't think it made quite the lasting impression the Bobbsey Twins did.

Bob Jones University in Greenville, South Carolina and Oral Roberts University in Tulsa have a combined total of about 7,000 enrolled students. Of course, not all students are named Bob. There are a few Robertas, too.

The letters, B-O-B, as you world travelers must already know, form the three-letter ID code for the Bora Bora airport.

Billy Bob's Huntin' & Fishin' is a Nintendo Gameboy game, probably by now obsolete, or should I say, "bobsolete?"

The bobwhite is an attractive, usually brown, ground-dwelling bird with a loud cheery song. It has great value as a destroyer of some 60 different species of weed seeds and 116 species of insects. So thank goodness, I think we can all agree, for the bobwhite.

In England, police are called Bobbies. And, "Bob's your uncle" is British slang meaning "simple as that." I happen to have an Uncle Bob who chews with his mouth open, but we call him Uncle Bawb, and you can tell he doesn't really fit into many polite discussions, much less this one. This is a shout out to you, Uncle Bawb! See you at Thanksgiving.

The BOB Motor Oil Recovery System is a handy garage gadget you'll want, along with some towels, when you get around to changing the oil in your car. You turn oil cans upside down and drain them on this device. The BOB in the name stands for "bottom of the barrel."

And after a tough afternoon changing oil, you might want to relax with Bob's Pickle Pops, made in Dallas, Texas. They're frozen pickle juice treats that, I understand, taste incredibly and exactly like they sound.

Have you had a Bob's burger in Washington State or tried BOB brand foods in Sweden? They make gourmet juices and jams. Bob's Candies are claimed, by the company, at least, to be the world's finest peppermints.

A Beer Named Bob is brewed by the Bitter Creek Brewing Company in Rock Springs, Wyoming. Meanwhile, Bob Moore and his Oregon company, Bob's Red Mill, offer vitamins and natural, whole grain products.

In the U.S., there are estimated to be more than 86,000 people named Bob. The name, Bobby, belongs to another 362,000. And there are 20,000 Robs. If you look up Robert, you'll find 4,941,502. That's more like it. Almost five million of 'em. In certain parts of the country, you can't throw a pickle pop without hitting a Bob.

There seem to be a lot of Bobs in the music industry: Bob Dylan, Bob Marley, Bob Seger, Bobby Vee, Bobby Vinton, Bobby McFerrin, Bobby Darin, and Bobby Rydell. I know I've left out a few, but you get the idea.

Only Bobs can join the exclusive Bob's Club, whose goal is to create the world's largest list of famous Bobs. Don't even think about joining it, unless you're one of the five million Bobs.

In 2011, neither Bob nor its variants made the top five male names for babies in any state. In fact, nowadays, a boy is more likely to be named Mason or Jacob or Elijah or Liam. And 25 years ago, in 1987, no Bobs made the top five list of male names, but there were a lot more Michaels and Christophers. Roberto showed up then, but its rank was 156, way below, such popular appellations as, oh, Travis and Zachary.

The name, Bob, didn't make the list of the ten oldest people in the world, either. But then again, the oldest people in history were all women. The youngest Bob is, oh wait, another Bobby has just been born while I'm speaking.

"Hi Bob!" was a college drinking game, in which TV viewers had to take a drink every time someone said, "Hi, Bob" on the Bob Newhart Show. Legend has it that no one ever completed the game before passing out.

And now that I've shared so much more than you ever wanted to know about Bobs, feel free to pass out yourself.

Changing My Life

I've noticed many people claim that certain things have changed their life. And they're not always pleased with the new life they have.

Now, hurricanes, tornadoes, and earthquakes that level your house can change your life, as can shipwrecks, aircraft disasters, terrorist activities, catastrophic injuries, and regrettable accidents with sulfuric acid perpetrated by your partner in the high school chemistry lab. I'm still feeling guilty about that one, Matthew. Honest.

But how much of an injury will rise to the level of changing your life? Obviously, a corn on your little toe wouldn't change your life, nor would a toothache. Even a broken arm wouldn't change your life as long as it was set properly. But losing an appendage altogether can change your life, especially if you used to rely on that appendage to play the piano or compete in the Olympics.

So, changing your life can be a matter of degree.

Could a rainy, blustery day change your life? It depends. If you were going to stay home anyway, it wouldn't matter. But if you decided not to attend a cocktail party where you would have met the love of your life, that could be life-changing, even if you never knew it. What's the moral of the story? Go to every cocktail party you're invited to, regardless of the weather. That's my advice.

You can get fired or sued or have your mother-in-law move in with you. Ditto for your grown children. All unforeseen and life-changing events. They can happen in a minute, believe me.

So far, I've focused on changing your life for the worst. But you can also change your life for the better.

Joining the Peace Corps, I've heard, is often a positive life-changing experience.

And so is doing well on the *America's Got Talent* show.

Having a baby or — even more significantly — having twins or triplets would certainly change your life. Children can certainly give a parent pleasure, but in the beginning it's at the expense of diapers, sleep, and rude stares by other patrons at your favorite restaurant. Later, of course, it can represent a significant financial commitment for food, clothing, education, therapy, and weddings. So, children can change your life, but be careful what you wish for.

On T.V. a formerly fat woman said that losing 75 pounds changed her life. I can see that. A loss of that many pounds could certainly increase her energy level, allow her to wear more attractive clothing, give her a better chance to win the Miss America contest, and perhaps even provide an alternative to entering a witness protection program.

Also, on a T.V. commercial, I learned some guy had a terrible car accident. That would qualify as an unfortunate change of life. But after consulting a personal injury lawyer, he got a $2 million settlement. He admitted that changed his life. I suppose those extra millions could go a long way in changing his life, especially if he was previously living in his aforementioned car.

Lottery winners might have the same reaction until they lose it all in a casino. That's a case of changing your life and then changing it back again.

The fact is, just about anything and everything you do has the potential of changing your life. Every morning represents another opportunity. And if that opportunity

192

changes a life for the worst, just hope it's someone else's life you've changed.

Civilization is Relative

During my recent trip to Ecuador, I had occasion to meet a gentleman who lives in the Amazon. He is a Huaorani (Hwă răh'ni), a people who have lived in their neighborhood for thousands of years, going back to the Stone Age. It is estimated that about 3,000 Huaorani exist. This new acquaintance of mine — call him Sam — stands about 4'9" high and has dark, but not leathery skin. He has black hair and not a touch of grey, probably because he lives a stress-free life. All he has to do is spear tasty looking animals and occasional enemies, and supervise his wife, who does everything else for the family. I was going to say household, but there is no house. No clothing, either.

Sam looks 50 years old, but I could be off by 20 years one way or the other. He seems pretty healthy, considering he has no access to a health care plan. His chest has fully developed muscles that make Arnold Schwarzenegger look like Woody Allen. He also has a hole in his earlobe big enough to slide an iPhone through.

I met Sam at a rather rustic resort near a town called Mindo, Ecuador, a couple of hours from Quito. I felt sorry for myself having to drive so far to get there until I learned that Sam had traveled by foot and canoe for three days from his home in the Amazon. Now, Sam didn't mention this fact to me directly, because he speaks only the Huaorani language, so his Spanish-speaking son did the translating.

Let me tell you about this rustic resort. A raging river borders the property, so to get across from the dirt road out of the town of Mindo, you have to ride precariously on this flat, wooden, one-person seat suspended by a rope and pulley. The seat has no sides to protect you from the raging river and its formidable boulders.

Once across the river and onto the property, I locate a common, open-aired-dining area — really just an unenclosed, platform and I find my wooden cabin — quite spacious, actually — with a grass thatched roof surrounded by a swarm of moths the size of pterodactyls. It could be a scene from Jurassic Park. No electricity but there are two candles and, believe it or not, a flush toilet. That's where technology ends.

I thought that was pretty rustic, especially for a place that calls itself a resort. But then I realized that the same location that represents a giant step backwards, civilization-wise, for me, is actually a great improvement for Sam, who was quite accustomed to living without a roof over his unkempt head. He doesn't have a satellite TV, either — not even basic cable — or a heater or an air conditioner or a refrigerator or a dish washer or even, let's face it, a roll of toilet paper.

How can he enjoy a Barry Manilow Christmas collection on CD while munching on microwave popcorn if he doesn't have a CD player or a microwave oven in the first place? The poor fellow doesn't have a toothbrush or a pair of Diodoro sneakers. He has survived, day after day for maybe 18,000 days, without a cell phone and without a full-length bathroom mirror. We take so many things for granted he doesn't even know exist.

I continued to feel sorry for Sam all the way up to the day I returned to civilization to discover my mortgage, my satellite TV bill, and two credit card payments were overdue. My electricity had been shut off, too, for the same reason.

Yes, civilization can be a relative thing. You have to feel sorry for people who don't know what they're missing.

Confessions of a Book Collector

When I was nine years old, I made a mistake I'm still paying for. The mistake resulted in having to add a 1,500 square foot addition to a house I used to own. Recently, my darling, long-suffering wife and I had to purchase a condo that's easily four times too big for just the two of us.

I could have decided to collect postage stamps or even jewelry, back when I was nine. Collections like those wouldn't have needed much space. But in 1958 I decided to buy a 35¢ paperback collection of science fiction short stories entitled, Men, Martians and Machines by Eric Frank Russell. (By the way, you can purchase the softcover book today online for three or four bucks or from a book dealer in Canada for $107.) I suppose I could have borrowed the book from my local library, but the cover was so attractive, I knew I had to own the book. Although 35¢ was not easy to come by for a pre-adolescent on a 25¢ weekly allowance, I thought the investment would be worthwhile.

Fast forward 56 years. I now have 11,278 books and a condo with six — count 'em, six! — bathrooms. My wife and I don't need three bathrooms apiece, but it's impossible to find a condo with one bedroom and a library big enough to hold 33 bookcases.

So, you see the magnitude of the mistake I made over half a century ago. My library has grown to include some thousand Sherlockian volumes, ten dozen annotated books, complete collections of the Best American Short Stories going back to 1915, O. Henry Award Prize Stories, books on inventors and their inventions, books on movie making, books on writing, and 700 books of limericks.

In my collection, I even have books on book collecting and the weirdoes who collect them. I especially enjoy books that refer to the "gentle madness" and the stories of obsessed people who bought multiple houses for their books or packed their house so tightly with books, there was no place to stand or lie down. When I read those stories, I can say, "I'm not that bad... yet."

Now that I have many complete sets of science fiction anthologies and collections of books by certain authors who specialize in mystery and popular fiction, I've entered into a new phase of book collecting. I'm on a quest to meet as many authors as I can and ask them to sign my copies of their books. I'm specializing in octogenarian authors, since I enjoy accomplishing tasks under time pressure.

In the last few years, I was able to meet the mystery short story writer, Ed Hoch, before he passed away. He was gracious enough to spend a couple of hours with me autographing a good portion of the 850 short stories he had published in the last four decades. I traveled to Rochester to meet him and his lovely wife.

Charles Harness was another find. He passed away about a decade ago at the age of 90, but not until he had signed 25 of his books for me in Maryland. Charles — he told me I could call him Charles — was an accomplished author in the '40s and '50s, but then decided to become a patent attorney and pursue that career for 40 years. And then he came back to writing science fiction. How's that for a life story? One of his later stories concerned a legal case in the future, when patent infringement became a crime punishable by death. I ask you, how can you not like an author who takes intellectual property violations so seriously?

J.P. Donleavy is turning out to be more elusive than I would have thought. He has what he calls a cottage but most of us would call a mansion, if not a castle, situated on 180 acres of land in Ireland. He doesn't answer my letters and, if this goes on, I'm afraid I'll have to pay him a personal visit. I don't know exactly where he lives, but how difficult can it be to find him? Ireland's a small country.

And speaking of reclusive authors, I once traveled 10 hours by car with a trunkful of books to meet up with a prolific author who values his privacy and requested that I not mention his name, not take his photo, not disclose his phone number, and not reveal the year of his birth. We spent a truly wonderful and memorable two hours discussing and signing 80 books. I can't tell you where he lives. In fact, I've probably said too much already.

I travel to book fairs and conventions around the country. This task I've set for myself is a breeze now that I live within a few miles of the south Florida independent book store, Books and Books. There, every week authors are invited to read some of their works and sign books.

But if the authors are mobile enough to visit a bookstore for a signing, they are nowhere near old enough for me.

Costly Comestibles

Previously, I investigated the most expensive items or objects one could purchase if he happened to win the lottery, which I intend to do any day now.

But it occurred to me that President Trump may stop by my place to visit, the next time he comes to Colorado. The chances of that happening are actually slightly less than winning the lottery, since I still haven't removed the Hillary signs on my lawn. In any case, I might as well be prepared for the visit.

I can't assume that Trump, or The Donald, as his few friends know him, will be satisfied with a bucket of fried chicken, with which he posed on his airplane during the election campaign.

So, I decided to find the most expensive victuals I could afford, pre-lottery. I'm now ready to offer our president some snacks from the top shelf of my pantry.

They include Alba truffles. Those winter white truffle products run up to $7,000 per pound. Truffles are rare, but they're basically mushrooms. The white ones are available only a couple of months of the year, almost exclusively from one part of Italy, where they used to be foraged by special pigs. There are fewer white truffles, and of lesser quality, every year.

White truffles have a unique aroma, a combination of newly plowed soil, fall rain, burrowing earthworms, and the pungent memory of lost youth and old love affairs, as it says on the package. One chef said, "The way truffles smell is disconcerting. It conjures up images of a locker room. But the aroma deceptively conceals their complex yet delicate taste. They are sublime."

Female — and only female — pigs were the original truffle seekers. Truffles apparently smell like testosterone to female swine, making them eagerly sought out. But there's a problem with swine. Pigs love to eat truffles and they don't want to give them up. So, dogs were trained to locate those delicacies. In fact, use of pigs to hunt truffles has been prohibited since 1985 because they damage the truffle beds in their zeal to get to the scent.

A network of 18,000 people hunts for truffles in Italy. A single truffle hunter with a dog can usually find a small amount — two or three ounces. So you can imagine the excitement when a single, 4.16 pound white truffle — the so-called "world's largest" — sold recently at a Sotheby's auction for $61,250 to a phone bidder in China. Can you imagine someone there wrestling that huge Italian snack with chopsticks?

But wait. That's not the most expensive white truffle. Dong Zhenxiang, chef-owner of top-rated Da Dong Roast Duck in Beijing, China, won an auction for a two-and-a-half pound truffle in Italy with a winning bid of $112,000. Pretty impressive for a mushroom.

Caviar and duck foie gras are logical choices for a meal with the president, but he's more of a meat and potatoes guy, I think. That's where Kobe steaks come in.

Kobe beef is prized for its tenderness and high degree of marbling. It has one of the greatest amounts of marbling of any steak.

I have to be careful that the steak I purchase is authentic Kobe beef. Beef outside Japan marketed as Kobe beef may be incorrectly labeled as Kobe beef. See, we always get back to trademarks. But only about 3,000 head of cattle may qualify as Kobe.

That helps explain its high price, which runs at least $150 per pound. In a restaurant, you can expect to pay $50 for a 4-ounce filet mignon. I may never experience that little appetizer. Another factor in raising the price of Kobe beef is the fact that heifers are massaged regularly with oil for about 20 minutes every day. The good news, if you're planning to raise Kobe cattle, is that you have to give these massages to each of your cows only between May and October to soften and better distribute the heifer's subcutaneous fat. If your heifer seems to have a reduced appetite, you can give her a bottle of beer to stimulate her digestive system, which may shut down due to her confinement in her pen. You wouldn't want to exercise her too much, since more muscle mass is not what you're looking for.

In Japan, all cattle can be tracked via a 10-digit number through every step of its entire lifecycle. That's the sort of trivia you've come to expect from my ramblings. I hope the president is appropriately impressed.

Dishonorable Discharge

What do Walt Disney and John Wayne have in common?

Rumor has it both men were dishonorably discharged or "DD" from the military.

But it turns out, John Wayne was exempted from service due to his family status and advanced age. He was 34 when Pearl Harbor was attacked. Actually, he toured military bases and was given an award for his service with the OSS in World War II.

Walt Disney did not receive a dishonorable discharge either, rumors to the contrary. He was rejected from the Army because he was too young to enlist in 1918 when he was only 16 years old. So, after unsuccessfully trying to enlist in the Canadian Army, he joined the American Ambulance Corps, a division of the Red Cross, by lying about his age.

In order to impose a dishonorable discharge, a military court must conduct a court martial, finding a soldier guilty of a serious military or civil crime, such as sexual assault, which can occur as a result of a variety of unlawful sexual activities, a topic for another day, you'll be gratified to learn.

I, myself, was in the Air National Guard. The closest I came to being dishonorably discharged was when I was first promoted. I sewed my Airman First Class stripe on upside-down. It wasn't meant to be an unpatriotic act, merely a frugal one: I wanted to avoid paying the 15¢ professional uniform alteration fee. But that was just a silly mistake. My drill sergeant and I had a good laugh over it. You can't get court marshaled just for being an incompetent and misguided tailor, can you?

Murder — the premeditated, intentional act of taking someone's life — is also a crime that can result in a dishonorable discharge. That's understandable, but manslaughter — the unintentional action or inaction that results in someone's death — can also lead to a dishonorable discharge, which hardly seems fair. I mean accidents happen.

While engaging in combat, deaths are not considered murder or manslaughter, but rather a casualty of war. However, the taking of a life of a soldier or civilian while not engaged in active combat can be murder or manslaughter, for which a dishonorable discharge can result.

Absent Without Official Leave, commonly known as going AWOL, refers to a soldier's departure from his or her assigned post or base with the intention of not returning to service. AWOL is usually used interchangeably with desertion, and is one of the strongest cases for a dishonorable discharge.

The majority of other illegal actions, such as drug abuse or domestic violence or sewing stripes on a uniform upside-down, usually do not lead to a dishonorable discharge, but they may cause a soldier to get a bad conduct discharge.

Some famous or infamous people have been dishonorably discharged. Lenny Bruce, the comedian, was one, as was François Truffaut, the film director, and William Calley, the officer who led the My Lai massacre.

Boxers appear to have anger management issues. Who would have thought? Hurricane Carter, the boxer who was convicted of triple murder, and Rocky Graziano, the middleweight boxing champ, are on the list.

John Dillinger, Public Enemy Number One for a while, was DD, as was Jerry Garcia of the Grateful Dead musical group.

Surprisingly, only one politician made the list: Harvey Milk, the openly gay San Francisco city supervisor. And speaking of Harveys, the infamous assassin, Lee Harvey Oswald, was also DD.

Writers can be problematical, too. There are no fewer than eight authors, novelists, and journalists who were DD. Frankie Lymon, the songwriting member of the Frankie Lymon and the Teenagers musical group and Edgar Allan Poe, of all people, were also dishonorably discharged. I suppose if a presidential candidate is DD, Donald Trump will let us know.

So far, no broadcast essayists have been dishonorably discharged from the military. Only time will tell if one is eventually DD from Weekend Radio.

Dreaming

Nowadays, I've lost the ability to remember things, concentrate on problems, and run 100 yards in less than a minute. But one of the things I *can* still do is sleep.

I think I inherited this particular super power from my father, who could fall asleep at a moment's notice. He could nod off on our living room couch in front of the T.V. or in the middle of a spirited conversation or a joke-telling session among his four children. Sometimes we kids would hear gentle snoring just as a punchline was delivered. He also traveled quite a bit and had the ability to fall asleep on one of those uncomfortable airplane seats before the plane even started to taxi down the runway.

I'm not quite as good as that, but I've been known to fall asleep shortly before my head hits my pillow.

And not only sleep, but dream.

I usually have very pleasant dreams, which is a good thing, since I sleep so much.

Unfortunately, like many people, I don't recall much of my dreams. That reminds me of a story. It seems this writer often had amazing dreams, but forgot them upon awakening. He complained to one of his friends that he often had great ideas for stories while sleeping, but lost them when he woke up.

"What you should try," his friend suggested, "is put a pencil and paper on a nightstand close to your bed. Also, set the alarm to go off in the middle of the night. That way, you'll wake up during one of your dreams and you'll remember what you were dreaming about. Just write it down and go back to sleep."

Sure enough, that night he set his alarm clock for 3:00 a.m. and placed a pad of paper and a pencil on his nightstand.

When the time came, the alarm went off, he woke up, groggily reached for his pencil and wrote down the idea he had dreamed about for a great story.

The next morning, he could hardly wait to see what he had written. Imagine his disappointment when he read his note, written in a scraggly hand: "A great idea for a story."

Now back to me. I may not remember the details, but I *do* know I dream of winning the lottery and conducting symphonic orchestras and writing a best-selling novel and eating delicious meals and floating down streams and flying and dating movie stars. You know, the standard things every healthy guy dreams about.

What I don't seem to be able to do is read or interpret letters and numbers or see myself in a mirror. Either I won't look like myself or my face will be blurry.

The way I heard it is, when we dream, the part of the brain responsible for logic and intellect shuts down, allowing us to accept crazy dream stuff as reality while at the same time inhibiting our ability to read or do arithmetic. So, trying to read something and not being able to is considered one of the signs that you're dreaming. Are you dreaming right now? No, you can't be, because you're reading this.

Here's another test to see if you're dreaming: look at the palms of your hands. If they're lined, you're awake; if they're smooth or disfigured, you're dreaming. And take a look at who's around you. If you're with strangers, you may be dreaming. If you're with people you know are dead, you're definitely dreaming.

Simple, isn't it?

Now that we've cleared all that up, I'm going to set my alarm clock.

Election Time – 2020

Unless you've been living under a rock for the last year or so, you know it's time to decide who should be our country's next president by voting on Tuesday. Your choices are limited to candidates who belong to two (or three or four) political parties.

But not so fast!

Did you know that If you have registered to vote, instead of checking or clicking on or punching your ballot, you can write in the name of a person who is not on the official ballot?

I humbly suggest you write my name on your ballot, and I'll tell you why.

I am a U.S. citizen, born in this country, and I have a birth certificate to prove it. I'm over 35 years old, but I'm younger than the two major candidates you know about. Well, just barely.

I haven't sent emails with classified information and, if I have, I haven't hidden any of them. Actually, no one has ever entrusted me with classified information, so that was an easy one.

I haven't started a university or built any buildings with my name on them. Now that I think of it, I haven't built any buildings, period. I don't have employees, but if I did, I would have paid them the amount we had agreed upon. I don't have a foundation, but if I did, I wouldn't give any donors an appointment at the State Department or promise any of them a job. And I wouldn't use the funds in the foundation to purchase a six-foot, two-inch portrait of myself or anyone else for that matter.

I don't have a racist bone in my body. I'm not prejudiced against women, Muslims, the handicapped, or judges of Mexican descent.

I occasionally wear a pants suit, just like all the candidates. But no one will make fun of my hair, since I'm bald.

I believe the White House is much bigger than my house, which would be an improvement, since I have a lot of books. I'm not too good at mowing the lawn, but I've never seen a president do that in front of the White House, anyway.

And I understand the White House chef can whip up a snack anytime, day or night. I'm already working on my list of late-night treats, but don't tell my future First Lady.

I don't have a slogan, like "Make America Great Again" or "Stronger Together," but I could work on that when crisscrossing the country in my jet, if I had one.

Finally, to paraphrase the recent words of a presidential candidate, by writing me in, what have you got to lose?

Erics

Over the years, I have befriended four unique individuals with only one thing in common: they are all named Eric.

Eric-the-Dentist is my best friend. We met in third grade at Public School 178 and we have stayed friends for the past 50 years. He is intelligent, well-read, and self-effacing, with a charming, Seinfeld-like personality. An accomplished pianist, he favors the repertoire of our parents' generation — Cole Porter and George Gershwin. We while away hours listening to CDs — played entirely too loudly — at his Long Island bachelor abode.

Eric-the-Physicist is a genius. Truly. Though he had a slight, anemic form, he was difficult to ignore in our technical college, where I met him. He frequently corrected our math and physics professors, approaching the blackboard with confidence, seizing the chalk from their hands, and proceeding to derive the differential equation du jour. Although he never graduated (due to a monumental lack of ability in foreign languages), he has a technical mind of the first order. For example, he helped design the lenses that make tiny LED displays visible on calculators. I once saw him repair a television in a motel, using just a mess kit knife. So, when I am inclined to dope out any problem in math, science, or logic, he's the first (and usually the last) one I call.

Eric-the-Jester could have been around during the Renaissance. His Robin Williams-like wit got him elected high school class clown. He has the sort of impish gleam in his eye that makes you nervous when he's near liquids, flames, or small children. His face and gangling physique are entirely at ease in front of a movie camera lens. He can play almost any part and is always willing to do so. I've made a number of amateur videos with him, and notice that we rarely shoot a second take. He taught himself to juggle and is now up to five clubs. He is not all physical, though. As an electrical engineer, his math and verbal skills allowed him to join Mensa, the high IQ society, where I met him.

Eric-the-Philosopher is the Eric whom I met most recently. Raised in rural Wyoming, as redundant as that sounds, showing great persistence, he got through four schools of higher education, eventually earning a Ph.D. He is now a professor of philosophy and author of textbooks on machine intelligence, analyzing such esoteric problems as, "Will silicon-based life-forms ever have a sense of humor and, if so, what will they find hilarious about us, their carbon-based creators?" His zany observations and bizarre approaches to problems are both refreshing and disconcerting. In many ways, he is the Richard Feynman of philosophy, exhibiting the same sort of iconoclastic irreverence and sense of wonder that leads, seemingly logically, to the most absurd, disturbing conclusions. I envy the undergraduates who get to enjoy his daily standup routines.

And so my collection of Erics continues. Like a baseball card collector, I seek the hard-to-find Erics — those whose quirks pique my interest. If I can attract enough of them, eventually I may be in a position to trade; but of course, I couldn't really part with any of them.

Everybody Should Go to Law School

As crazy as this sounds, I think everybody should go to law school. I know what you're thinking: we have too many lawyers already; an entire society of lawyers would be like a science fiction horror movie come to life. But hear me out, please, before you call the men in the white coats.

Law school can be an enlightening experience. It requires only three years after you graduate college — four if you go to night school, which law schools like to call "part time" or "the evening division." Really, in the great scheme of things, what are three or four years of your life? You've already probably spent more time doing unimportant things, like spending quality time with your family. You'd hardly miss three or four years. Trust me; I'm a lawyer.

Here's another benefit of going to law school: you get to read about all sorts of crimes and bad behavior. In a way, it's a TV reality show without the pictures or the sound effects.

I know three good reasons to attend law school, even if you never want to practice law a day in your life.

First, a legal education will teach you how to negotiate. That's an important skill, since we all negotiate dozens of times a day. When I wake up in the morning, I have to negotiate with my wife who will get to brush his or her teeth first. Then we negotiate who will prepare breakfast, what the breakfast will be, who will walk down the driveway to retrieve the newspaper, who will use the last five drops of

213

milk in his or her coffee, and who will decide where to meet for lunch.

That's the typical morning routine that I engage in on Saturdays and Sundays alone. During the work week, I negotiate with business associates, with retail store employees, with bank tellers, with grocery store cashiers, and with taxi drivers, not to mention dealing with a fairly long list of requests demanded by my children, of course.

So, you see how valuable it is to have good training in negotiating tactics.

Here's the second reason I think a law school education is helpful: you get to know how to get around the law.

Take the simple "do not enter" sign. How often have you seen that sign and been deterred from going where you want to go? How often have you had to pack up your suitcase and rush out of a hotel room before the 11:00 a.m. checkout time? How often have you had to pay your income taxes? (Just kidding, all you IRS agents out there.)

How often have you heard someone say, "you can't do that" or "we can't do that" or "nobody can do that?" When you're a lawyer, you don't blindly accept those statements; you take them as a personal challenge.

Going to law school means never having to take "no" for an answer, with the possible exception of when an aforementioned IRS agent says it. There's almost always a way to accomplish your goal if you learn how to approach every problem as if there must be a solution. Of course, that's what lawyers get paid to help you with, but if you get the education and you can develop the correct mindset, most of the time you won't need no stinkin' lawyer to help you out. Look at the money you'll save by attending law school for yourself.

Which brings me to the third advantage of going to law school and perhaps the most important reason I think everybody should have a legal education: you learn when you should call a lawyer. You may think that's a trivial reason for spending so many hours reading cases about plaintiffs and defendants, but you'd be surprised how often people go to a lawyer too late in the game.

For example, in real estate only a small percentage of home buyers consult a lawyer before they sign what the real estate agents call a "binder," but which lawyers know is a contract. Turns out, the lawyer they select has one hand tied behind his or her back, since the client has already agreed to certain terms and conditions and forfeited some options in that binder agreement. Usually, it would have cost the buyer the same to engage the lawyer before the binder was signed as after.

In the patent business, where I spend most of my time, I can't tell you how often inventors approach me more than a year after they've publicly disclosed their invention. That's a shame. The patent law states that an inventor cannot obtain a patent unless the invention has been publicly disclosed, if at all, for less than a year. If the inventor had made the appointment with me a year earlier, he might have obtained a patent. But because he didn't know when to call a lawyer, he's out of luck. That's why Mr. Rubik never received a patent for Rubik's Cube, by the way.

So, there you have it. Everybody should go to law school to learn how to negotiate, learn not to take "no" for an answer, and learn when to call a lawyer. Luckily, it's never too late to go to law school, so start saving up for the tuition now. I should have mentioned that earlier.

Hey, tuition fees may be negotiable. If you look for loopholes, as we say in the legal biz, and you don't take "no" for an answer, you're already on your way to being a lawyer. See how easy that is?

Excess

The 21st century is an age of excess. I bought a car that can go way faster than I have the nerve to drive. And the speedometer also includes speed markings in kilometers, which makes the speed look 62% faster. Oh, and there are seven — count 'em SEVEN — digits on the odometer. That's over a million miles in one car, or two round trips to the moon. Who drives that far? A million miles. Sheeesh. I'm lucky if I can get to a tenth of that — one hundred thousand miles — without my engine blowing up, like it's already done in a couple of my previous cars.

The point is, my speedometer and my odometer and my car itself have much greater capacity than I need. It also has four exhausts, which is one more than the space shuttle used to have. And it's not just the car that exceeds the comfort range of most humans.

I also have a computer with a memory that's the envy of every other computer on my block. If I write a 300-page novel every other day and store it in the memory of my computer, I won't need to get another computer for a million years; well, at least 850 thousand years.

The folks who make hot dog rolls sell them in packages of eight, even though hot dogs themselves come in packages of six. I've been to many barbeques, but darned if I've ever heard someone request an extra roll for her hot dog.

My wristwatch is accurate to a hundredth of a second, but I can't change my habit of telling my friend I'll meet him for lunch "around noon." The watch is guaranteed to work up to 200 meters under water. It would have to be quite a downpour to result in that much water on my street. And if I did find myself 200 meters under water someday — the equivalent of over two football fields deep — I don't think checking the time of day would be my highest priority.

The hot water in my kitchen sink is capable of scalding the feathers off a chicken. But all I need is warm water to rinse plates before the dishwasher takes over.

As long as I'm in the kitchen, let me tell you about my new microwave oven. It exceeds my desire or capacity to use it. Its keyboard has about 90 settings, so I can thaw, simmer, and overcook. I can start the process immediately or I can instruct the machine to start cooking 6 days and 23 hours from now. I can vary the heat and the time for each of up to 999 cooking steps. If I google a microwave recipe someday, for example, maybe I'll prepare pheasant under glass in that unit. But like most of us, now I use it just to boil water or make popcorn.

Speaking of popcorn, we all know that movie theaters now sell large, gargantuan, and humongous sizes of popcorn. But did you know that big box stores sell Cheerios in a cardboard box that's 6 by 8 by almost 14 inches high? Who has a family that big? And who has room for a box that size in their kitchen? I would need a separate parking space for that thing.

My TV has a sound system that can be cranked up enough decibels to shatter my windows. I could be deaf as a post and still not miss a syllable. And the size of that TV! Gosh. The images are bigger than life. I get nightmares sometimes when I try to sleep after seeing Nancy Grace's disapproving smirks two and a half feet high. The TV has dimensions that overwhelm my bedroom or any other room in my house. In fact, if I didn't have an exterior wall, you could see it from space.

Feeling Bad After

I have cheated. I have sinned. I have eaten an apple.

How strange it is to feel guilt when I stray from an arguably bizarre diet. It's not as if I'm engaging in an extramarital affair, pushing drugs, harming innocent people, under reporting my income to the IRS, or even rolling through a stop sign. What engenders this guilty feeling is merely chomping down on a piece of fruit that, after all, most people believe is healthy. How little they know.

A few months ago, I began a low carbohydrate diet to lose weight. Carbohydrates, as some people know and I soon learned, are more than just pasta, starch, and sugar and are present in bread, cereal, bagels, potatoes, ice cream, beer, candy, milk, fruit, most nuts, and all too many vegetables.

The list of foods that I am prohibited from eating is long indeed. In fact, basically I am restricted to walking the perimeter of the supermarket — the meat and cheese sections, unable to perambulate the aisles themselves. Even diet food aisles are off limits. By the same token, certain victuals are inherently and surprisingly low in carbs. For example, the diet permits and even encourages fat- and cholesterol-laden goodies such as bacon, eggs, mayonnaise, butter, and, of all things, fried pork rinds.

According to low carb and, without going into the scientific details, sugar and starch that are not used by the body by running a marathon for example, are stored as fat. Therefore, by eliminating carbs, the body is forced to use its own, previously-stored fat.

Sounds simple doesn't it? Proponents of these diets even claim that, with appropriate vitamin supplements, a person becomes not only lighter, but healthier. My cholesterol actually decreases, as do blood sugar, uric acid levels, and sugar in the blood. Go figure. It's an upside-down world. Lobster and shrimp scampi drenched in butter with a generous portion of filet mignon is perfectly fine. Not a gram of carbs on the whole plate. But a simple baked potato, even unadorned, is verboten.

I can have cream cheese and lox, but I can't spread them on anything. I can have turkey but no stuffing, roast beef but no gravy, ranch salad dressing but no peas, no carrots. An olive, but not the martini in which it is submerged. Heavy cream, butter, and sour cream but no margarine or milk, not even skimmed milk. I cannot enjoy peanuts, almonds, or filberts, but fatty macadamias are perfectly acceptable.

Fat and grease are no longer to be avoided. I can sit at a restaurant with a companion who is enrolled in a low-fat, calorie-counting program — why must dieters use euphemisms? — and eat almost everything that he doesn't. In that way, while complimenting each other on our resolve and progress, we also complement each other's cuisine.

To sum up this peculiar diet, apothegmatically, I can eat only what is bad for me. I have taken to ordering familiar foods and dismembering and excising the contaminants to have only what I consider harmless ingredients. Pizza, for example, is detoxified after I discard the crust and the sauce, leaving only the toppings: spices and mozzarella. I have chili without beans — less satisfying but more Texan. I pluck out the offending and ubiquitous croutons from my salad. I must say, though, that consuming an egg salad sandwich on the run, sans bread, can be messy to say the least.

Morality can be awfully subjective, sometimes defined only by the structure of the organization to which we belong. To those outside of the faith, my feelings of remorse must appear absurd. Hemingway's comment in Death in the Afternoon rattles around in my mind: "what is moral is what you feel good after and what is immoral is what you feel bad after."

As a corollary, it appears that what is moral to one person, especially in food consumption, as it turns out, may not be moral to another. To a Hindu, for ex-ample, a hamburger is sacrilege. Melt a slice of cheese over it and it becomes unkosher. Pope 23rd's opinion notwithstanding, a devout Catholic would never dream of eating one with or without cheese on a Friday during Lent. For a low carb believer, on the other hand, the burger minus the bun of course is perfectly fine. It is the seemingly innocuous banana, however, that is unpardonably sinful.

Feeling Superior

I can't be the only one who doubts his normalcy, can I? Don't others want to be sure they're accepted, especially by strangers? Isn't that why people wear popular designer clothing, have their hair styled in the fashion of the day, and don't chew with their mouth full?

Perhaps I'm more sensitive than others when it comes to fitting in. My approach goes beyond checking that my hair — as little as I have — is in place and my fly is zipped up. Whenever I pass a mirror, of course I check to see I have no egg or other foreign substances on my face.

But I am compelled to go further to ensure I'm as normal as they come. In fact, I cheat. I befriend people who are clearly not mainstream. The weirder my friends are, the more normal I feel.

"I may not be a sophisticated movie star," I think, "but at least I'm not as ugly, obnoxious, or insane as he is!"

For example, one of my friends — I call him Oscar, as in Oscar Levant — has a nervous habit of stroking his clean-shaven face with his hands. He vigorously rubs his eyes, his cheeks, and his mouth like he's sanding unfinished furniture. He usually performs this flesh sanding while talking. Speaking of which, he has a habit of taking a big bite of food and chewing it in the middle of his own sentence. This prevents others from jumping in with their point of view, since they would clearly be interrupting him. Only he is rude enough to interrupt himself, you see. It's as if he has a choice between finishing his thought and finishing his meal and he decides to do both. He typically sounds something like this: "I bought a hundred shares of IBM at 75..." — pause; continue unintelligibly — "... but it hasn't moved a point in three months!"

I have another friend I call Dale, as in Dale Earnhardt. He often proposes to give me a ride in his 1978 Dodge Dart, which is a gracious enough offer, but he never, never drives faster than 35 miles per hour. The experience for me goes from terrifying when we're on crowded side roads to boring when we're on the highway. Except for the vehicles whizzing by on both sides of the car, the whole world seems to slow down when I'm his passenger.

Another of my friends — I call him Ludwig — has a very large head of thick, pure white hair. It grows straight out of his scalp like a fibrous cauliflower. His forehead overhangs his eyes, so the general impression is Beethoven on the loose. As we walk downtown, I expect him to break into the chorus of "Ode to Joy." And I can tell that a number of other pedestrians expect that, too.

Finally, I know a woman I call Chatty, which is more polite than Motor Mouth. She has a truly fantastic ability to speak without taking a breath. You probably know the type: there's never a good time to insert a comment because her monologue drifts seamlessly from topic to topic. She is a female Robin Williams on steroids. I believe she can talk faster and longer, without inhaling, than any other human in history.

So you see, surrounded by these friends, through no fault of my own, I appear to be relatively straight and narrow, sober as a judge, and — did I say "relatively?" — solid as a rock.

Generals

Remember that TV show called "The $100,000 Pyramid" where the contestants had to guess a category based on examples that their partner gave them? I don't have a hundred thousand dollars on me at the moment, but I'm so sure you wouldn't figure this out, that I'll give you my house if you do.

Here goes. I'll give you a list of famous people's first names in alphabetical order and you tell me what they have in common:

Bantz
Barksdale
Berton
Binford
Brehon
Burwell

Did you get what they all have in common yet? Okay, I'll help you out with a few more first names of famous people in the field:

Carter
Coral
Cortland
Courtney
Creighton
Ferdinand
Lucian

Still not enough of a clue? Okay, here is the final group of first names of famous people in the same profession:

Lyman
Malin
Mastin
Payton
Tasker
Volney
Walton

I won't keep you in suspense any longer. These are first names of people whom you wouldn't think are particularly modest. They're United States military generals. Notice I didn't give you a few names that would have given the answer away, like Omar, Norman, Wesley, Colin, and Dwight.

Here are some of the full names:

General Bantz J. Craddock,the Commander of the United States European Command.

General Carter F. Ham, the commanding general, 7th United States Army.

Brigadier General Coral Wong Pietsch, U.S. Army.

Major General Mastin M. Robeson, Commander, U.S. Marine Corps Forces Special Operations Command.

General Creighton W. Abrams, Jr., former Chief of Staff of the U.S. Army.

Malin Craig (1875–1945) the general who served in World War I and, later, as Chief of Staff of the U.S. Army.

General Tasker H. Bliss, Chief of Staff during WW I.

Needless to say, you can track down all of these generals and more on the Internet. So, there's no reason to consult a book of babies' names in anticipation of the next child to be born in your family.

Going to the Movies

Now I remember why I like the modern movie-going experience. It's not just because theaters are heated or air-conditioned, depending on the outside temperature, or because stadium seating allows me to have an unobstructed view of the entire screen, or because the plush, cushioned, reclining, double-wide seats with armchair cup holders are comfortable enough to snooze through the boring parts of the film, which I have been known to do, sometimes multiple times in the course of one movie. Dancing with Wolves comes to mind.

The first movie theater was constructed in 1895 in Berlin. There was no need for a multiplex then, since only a handful of movies existed. In the last 25 years, while the number of drive-in movies has shrunk from over 2,000 to barely 300, the number of indoor movie screens open to the public in North America has almost doubled from 20,000 to 39,000.

Modern movie theaters still have some drawbacks, like the price of admission and the price of, well, everything at the concession stand. And I'm not particularly fond of my fellow moviegoers in the audience coughing, sneezing, rustling, mumbling, and crying, especially during the boring parts of the film when I'm often trying to catch up on my sleep.

But those inconveniences are nothing compared to a recent experience I had in a very old theater that should have been condemned and, for all I know, actually was. It was a dismal afternoon with rain clouds threatening and I had a couple of hours to kill. I entered the theater with a recently-purchased, but stale bag of popcorn.

Well, I thought, at least I won't disturb anyone with my crunching. You see, I'm the sort of person who sees glasses half full.

Only two of the rows had a complete set of undamaged seats, the remaining ones looking like Godzilla had leaped from the screen and trampled them to bits. Fortunately, the theater was almost empty, so I had my pick of one of the few intact seats.

After a couple of false starts, the movie finally achieved lift-off and, despite speakers that had obviously seen better days, I was able to understand most of the dialogue.

It was halfway through the movie that I experienced a delightfully unexpected phenomenon. The scene included a man and a woman caught in a sudden cloudburst. The couple ran for cover, but not before the lovely actress was drenched from her feet to her bedraggled hair. The scene was so realistic, I actually felt raindrops bounce off of my bald head.

Wow, I thought, this is incredible; an immersion experience. I had heard of experimental, sensorama theaters in the 1960s that had tilting and shaking seats and introduced wind and aromas into the audience. Of course, lately we have 3-D movies and stereo sound, but this was the first I knew of water squirted from above onto an unsuspecting audience. I thoroughly enjoying being part of the action on screen, feeling drops of water while identifying with the drenched actors.

But then reality set in. The scene changed to a sunny day in an open field and I was still getting wet in the theater. It was only then, I'm embarrassed to admit, that I realized the thunderstorm outside hadn't ended. I could still hear faint thunder while water continued to drip from a leaky roof.

I didn't bother to complain to the manager, because I was ashamed to confess I sat under the hole in the roof for a full 15 minutes. The experience was so memorable, frankly, I returned the next day and took my previous seat. But as luck would have it, it was a sunny day.

You can imagine my disappointment. At least I had a darn good nap.

Have You Got an Egot?

I make amateur movies. And I, like everyone else who makes movies, amateur or professional, thinks his next movie can win an Oscar award. I guess composers and singers think they're one song away from winning a Grammy, too.

But let's face it: almost anyone can win an Oscar. The real question is how can I win an award in more than one field? Or better yet, how can I win all four major competitive, not honorary awards, one in each category – TV, music, movies, and plays? I wouldn't be the first one to win an EGOT, which stands for Emmy, Grammy, Oscar, and Tony award. Actually 15 people have won that grand slam. You can find them on the Internet under EGOT, along with the TV program, the song, the movie, and the play they won their respective awards for, what year they won each award, how old they were, and how long a time period it took them to complete the set of all four awards. On the list are Mel Brooks, John Legend, Andrew Lloyd Webber, Mike Nichols, Whoopi Goldberg, Tim Rice, Marvin Hamlisch, and Audrey Hepburn.

Richard Rodgers was the first person to win an EGOT in 1962. It took 15 more years before the next person won it. Guess who that was? You're right! Helen Hayes. She won it in 1977, 45 years after her first award, the 1932 Oscar for the movie, *The Sin of Madelon Claudet*, which I'm sure all of you have seen. Forty-five years is the longest time span of any EGOT winner between her first and fourth awards. Helen was the first woman to win it, but Rita Moreno was right behind her in the same year. Just 14 years later, the next winner, John Gielgud, made the list. He was 87 when he won it.

So, you can see it's pretty rare for an entertainment artist to win an EGOT. That's exactly why I'm shooting for it. I think it's important to aim high, think big, and convince yourself that anyone can win an Oscar.

Independent Day

Independence Day wasn't made a federal holiday until 1941, so the oldest of us have been celebrating the 4th of July officially for only 73 years.

I like Independence Day more than most other holidays, and here's why. First, unlike Christmas, I don't have to go into debt buying presents. And unlike Thanksgiving, I don't have to eat turkey or, worse yet, leftover turkey.

I get to go to sleep at a reasonable time, well before midnight, unlike on New Year's Eve.

I can always tell it's not Valentine's Day, because I'm not expected to buy flowers that will wilt, cards to be discarded, or candy to rot teeth and distort girlish figures. The 4th of July is the one day per year that some of us have an excuse to buy beer. The rest of us don't really need an excuse, I imagine.

Hardly anyone wears green, like on St. Patrick's Day, or parades around in a spring bonnet or a Halloween costume. And speaking of parades, on Independence Day, I don't have to attend a Columbus Day parade, no matter how cold, damp and dismal the weather.

The 4th of July doesn't have religious undertones either, like Easter, Passover, or Ramadan.

Independence Day commemorates the founding of our country, so it's arguably more important than Hallmark holidays like Mother's Day or Mother-in-Law's Day, which was started only in 2002, by the way, and is celebrated, for want of a more accurate word, on the 4th Sunday in October.

On the 4th of July, I'll be darned if I have to engage in trivial or superstitious activities, like rooting for a groundhog's shadow. All that's expected of me is inanely to wave a sparkler for a minute.

It's the only holiday in or around the summer that isn't somber like Memorial Day or slightly remorseful, for various reasons, like Labor Day. Father's Day hardly counts, since it's a lot more meaningful to children and grandchildren than it is to most fathers.

No, Independence Day is truly an independent day, set apart from all other holidays, epitomizing freedom. I'm really not forced to do anything. I don't even have to be sociable. I can have a cookout and invite friends or relatives, but I don't have to. I can watch fireworks, but I don't have to do that, either. I suppose I can even have fruit cake or eggnog, but I really don't know anyone who does.

Is it Worth It?

I've noticed that it can take a lot of time and effort to accomplish certain things, and I've noticed that, in an unbelievably short time, those accomplishments can be consumed, used up, destroyed, or — in the case of radio essays — simply ignored. Sometimes it hardly seems worth it.

It can take four or more years for an athlete to train for an Olympic event like running the 100-meter dash, but barely nine seconds to actually win the race. Sure, he or she could train for the 26-mile marathon, instead, and it will take about two hours to run it successfully, but even that doesn't seem like it's worth the effort. Four years of training for a two-hour event? The guy could have attended medical school in the same time.

It sometimes takes me three hours to prepare a delicious, nutritious dinner. That's not including the time, overnight, when the meat must marinate or the bread must rise. My family can devour a carefully prepared meal like that in less time than it takes to ignore a TV commercial.

Take house cleaning. Scrubbing floors, washing dishes, making the beds, and dusting are thankless jobs, when I consider how soon I'll be doing it again.

But just when I'm feeling sorry for myself and for all of my unappreciated work, I remember those ice sculptors who work so diligently carving birds and fish and cartoon characters, even though they must know spring is around the corner. Or worse yet, I think of the people who make elaborate, detailed sand castles on the beach, knowing, I'm pretty sure, that the ocean tide will come in as inevitably as I will receive reminders from the IRS when I forget to file my income taxes.

What must it be like for someone to begin a project knowing that it has an expiration date, a time, in fact, that is preciously close to the time that person started the project? I'm not talking about lasting works, like bridges or buildings or potholders. I'm talking about things that, by their nature, will melt or dissolve or be consumed entirely in a very short time.

I wonder which endeavor requires the most preparation versus the life of the product or the event? As I said, I wonder about that, but frankly, I can't afford to spend much time ruminating... it just isn't worth it.

It's My Dog's Life

The idiom "it's a dog's life" was coined in the 16th century to mean an unpleasant, miserable, wretched, subservient existence. That's because dogs back then were put to work as watch dogs or hunting animals and many times, they were ill-fed and mistreated.

But more recently, now that dogs are rarely expected to work for middle-class Americans, "it's a dog's life" implies a pampered existence with little or no responsibilities.

My own Chihuahua, Cashew, for example, has it made. She has the house to herself during work days and can be found resting or sleeping on one of her four doggie beds on the verboten living room couch when she's not playing with her toys or dining on the free range rotisserie chicken from the gourmet supermarket I've cut into bite-sized pieces or going for a ride in my car, sitting on my lap with her head out the window on the way to a posh park for a walk in a better neighborhood than ours.

The things little Cashew doesn't concern herself with include: earning a living, deciding whom to vote for, leaving a small carbon footprint by recycling when she thinks of it, balancing her budget, clipping grocery coupons, analyzing the Najdorf variation of the classic Sicilian defense in chess, calling her mother on Mother's Day, tipping the mailman, dressing up to attend a symphony concert, or choosing a seat on an airplane and hoping it's not in front of a seat occupied by an overactive three-year-old.

She never curses, even when she walks into misplaced furniture in the dark, and she doesn't have to remember where her car is located in the parking lot. She doesn't wait in the drive-in line at a fast food restaurant behind a person who is attempting to pay for McNuggets with every last penny that's stuck in the seat cushion.

Cashew doesn't send her shirts out to the cleaners, doesn't agonize over the best bargain in deodorants, and doesn't have to come up with excuses not to attend boring cocktail parties. She doesn't set her alarm clock, program her thermostat, check her email, update a shopping list, calculate an appropriate gratuity for her restaurant server, mail holiday cards, or have to locate a florist clear across town a few minutes before closing on Valentine's Day.

She doesn't have to keep up with the latest styles of clothing, footwear, or head covering. She can take or leave a Louis Vuitton handbag or a Hermés matte crocodile biking bag. Fine jewelry and cheap plastic are pretty much indistinguishable for her. A Timex wristwatch and a Patek Caliber timepiece mean the same to her, since she can't tell time, analogue or digital. Likewise, she doesn't see the advantage of Montblanc luxury writing instruments over BIC pens. She is completely unconcerned about the price of gasoline and — now that I think of it — the price of just about everything else. She doesn't purchase her friends' grown children wedding gifts from stores at which they're registered. She couldn't care less about the difference between a high value work of art and the scribblings of my two-year-old grandson.

She doesn't volunteer to work for non-profit causes or donate money to the poor, the hungry, or the homeless. She seems inured to television ads to raise funds for abused animals. She doesn't donate to her alma mater and she doesn't have a retirement account. She hasn't filed income tax since I've known her. She doesn't give a hoot about

237

belonging to any club or organization, and she isn't troubled about missing a meeting thereof.

She never has to control her road rage on the exit ramp when some jerk cuts ahead of her in the line in which she's been patiently idling for 15 minutes. She doesn't have to schedule car inspections, or choose between used Volkswagen vans and shiny new Lamborghini Venenos. And of course, when she's in public, she doesn't have to refrain from farting.

Cashew also seems to be oblivious to the meaning of life and has never set paw in a church or synagogue. Heaven holds no allure for her, as far as I can see. She doesn't seem to be aware that she will die. Eventually, while most of us have to write a will, pay life insurance premiums, choose a funeral home, and get our affairs in order, Cashew will transition into the afterlife without a care in the world.

It may sound as if I'm jealous of the life my little dog leads, especially when she flips on her back and beckons me with her front paws to scratch her belly. I don't know if "jealous" is a fair adjective that describes my feelings. I merely believe she gets way too many perquisites in exchange for simple, unconditional love.

It's the Thought, Indeed

A few years ago, I had occasion to try to purchase a gift for my wife. Frankly, I don't remember the nature of the occasion. Probably her birthday or our wedding anniversary, since those are the only two events that she ever forces me to celebrate. I do believe the occasion was insignificant and is now irrelevant.

The point is, I failed. I had made the supreme effort of remembering to buy the gift — some gold trinket as I recall — and even of traveling to the jewelry store, but my timing was off. By the time I got to my destination, the place was closed for the night. Apologetically, I returned home.

"Honey," said I, "my intention was to buy you a large and lovely [whatever], but the shop was closed by the time I got there. So sorry. I really wanted to do something special for you, since I knew it was your [whatever], but fate had other plans. What can I do?"

Her reaction caught me off guard. At first, I thought she was reaching out to strike me, but she actually smiled and patted my shoulder consolingly.

"Oh, poor dear," she said. "It's all right. Things like that happen. It's not your fault."

"But..."

"I don't mind at all. The important thing is it's the thought that counts."

How many times had I heard that trite apothegm? It must be true. How else to explain the brisk sales every year of cheap trophies that proclaim "World's Greatest Mom" or "Number 1 Dad?"

In the years since that embarrassing episode, numerous other situations have arisen in which I have not been able to fulfill my gift-giving obligations. Once, a snow storm thwarted my efforts. Another time my car wouldn't start. In seeming anticipation of my request, a pottery shop sold the last object of my desire to someone else. Yet another time, I had left my wallet at the office. I once traveled 14 miles only to find a joint had relocated.

All of these excuses are due to circumstances beyond my control. The would-be recipients typically and graciously dismiss their disappointments with a wave of their hand. In fact, I can't remember one person who has gone through what is becoming a routine who didn't forgive me. Most seem to be at least as happy with the thought as they would have been with the gift, which rarely matches expectations, at least in my case.

What a propitious phenomenon. As for my wife, nowadays she seems to be less interested in what I might have bought than curious to discover what my excuse will be. I have made a minor career out of this practice, as it turns out, unintentionally at first, but now with considerably more scienter. What started out as a serendipitous incident is now S.O.P.

Recently, it occurred to me that no one has ever asked me to prove my story. And how could they? Here I am, obviously humiliated and mortified, standing before them naked, but for my shield of well-intentioned bungling. Hardly the time to risk crushing my fragile ego with an inquisition.

No, my story and I inevitably escape unscathed.

It also occurred to me that I no longer heard comments like, "You shouldn't have," as the gift recipient glanced furtively around the room to find an inconspicuous place in which to stow my latest knickknack. Increasingly, people seem to harbor genuine relief that I am empty handed. My loved ones appear to be quite happy with my unconventional behavior.

Maybe it's my imagination but I'm sure my observations were objective, guilt assuaging notwithstanding.

So, I asked myself, why not go directly to the explanatory story stage? Why not skip the planning-to-buy-the-gift stage — it's the hardest part, anyway — and the circumstances-beyond-my-control stage, and jump right to the here's-what-happened-I'm-so-sorry stage?

I am only slightly ashamed to admit that, along the way, I am sometimes tempted to inflate the value of the gift I'm not delivering. A harmless prevarication under the circumstances. Indeed, I believe I am much better at coming up with credible-sounding stories for all occasions than I ever was at selecting presents.

It's very efficient, I must say. I've taken the time I would have devoted to deciding on and attempting to acquire an inappropriate gift and spent it instead on fabricating a plausible story.

And so, with all due regret to the flower, candy, and greeting card industries, I share this advice with my fellow, well-meaning gift-givers: just think.

Itsy Bitsy Baker Street Journal

I subscribe to an interesting publication that you may not have heard about. The number of readers of this publication is barely greater than the number of contributors. In fact, the motto of the *Baker Street Journal* — that's the publication for Sherlock Holmes scholars — used to be: "Never has so much been written by so many for so few."

You wouldn't think there would be much to write about what some unenlightened people think is a fictional detective whose best cases were solved around 1895. But boy, would you be mistaken. There's worldwide Sherlockian interest — an industry, really — that includes or produces novels, articles, cartoons, poems, songs, plays, stories, annotations, satires, horse races, trips to moors and graveyards, coffee table books, movies on DVDs, musicals, web sites, and assorted esoteric memorabilia like coffee cups, lapel pins, magnifying glasses, tobacco pipes, capes, and life-sized sculptures.

Contributors to the *Baker Street Journal* — or BSJ, as we Sherlockians call it — are often scholars who analyze Sherlock Holmes and Victorian society, customs, and motivations. Why did the dog do nothing in the night-time, for instance, when a stranger came into a stable and stole a horse? And how many times per day did London postmen deliver mail to businesses? (The answer is as many as 10 times per day.) And did it snow in London on February 23,

1886? And why were so many of Sherlock's clients named Violet?

Over the years, writers have speculated that Dr. Watson, Sherlock's faithful companion and roommate, was a woman, and that Sherlock himself was really a computer, and that occasionally Sherlock's older brother, Mycroft, was the British government. (Okay, that part's not speculation.) And that the evil Professor Moriarty had one or maybe two brothers, all of them named James — sort of the George Foremans of the archenemy crowd.

Sherlock, some of us believe, actually met or crossed single sticks with Sigmund Freud, Jack the Ripper, Tarzan, Fu Manchu, Dracula, the Phantom, Dr. Who, James Bond, Arsène Lupin, Karl Marx, Gandhi, and the Phantom of the Opera.

Discussion groups, sometimes called scions, meet in members' homes from Antarctica to Zambia. By the way, the Antarctica scion is appropriately called the Penguins of Antarctica. These groups remind me of Bible study groups, but in this case our Bible is what we call the Canon — the 56 short stories and 4 short novels that bear the name, Arthur Conan Doyle.

Sherlockians are fond of saying things like, "I hear of you everywhere," and "you see, but you do not observe," and "when you have eliminated the impossible, whatever remains, however improbable, must be the truth."

But they never, ever say "Elementary, my dear Watson." That's because that phrase — perhaps the most famous one attributed to Sherlock — does not appear in the Canon. Sherlock never said it. You could look it up, which I suggest you do, since "it is a capital mistake to theorize before one has data."

Leveling

I'm a pretty smart fellow. All my relatives tell me so. And I tell them they're pretty smart, too. So we have to believe each other. But sometimes I'm not smart enough, especially when an acquaintance is smarter than I am. Now I don't want to appear to be a dummy, so I've developed a few techniques over the years to hide my ignorance or, as I like to think, to appear smarter.

This leveling started with a friend named Davey who was half a year younger than I was. I taught him how to play chess. I was then six years old. I'll take credit for being a good teacher, because he soon became so adept, he won games regularly. In fact, he went on to be one of the best seventh grade chess players in the city of New York and one of his games was even published in the *New York Times*.

We used to play chess quite a bit. In order to even my chances of winning, he often consented to playing blindfolded while I was allowed to see the chess board. He still beat me.

We would usually play in his kitchen with the radio playing. Here's what I discovered, unbeknownst to Davey: when the radio played rock and roll, he would always win the games. But when the radio played classical music, I would occasionally battle him to a draw. Obviously, Beethoven was able to break Davey's concentration.

That was the first time I was able to level the playing field, literally and figuratively. If I wanted to have a fighting chance to win a chess game with Davey, I had to play classical music. I called it the Ludwig Effect.

The next time I had to claw my way out of my normal intellectual morass was professionally. One of my clients named Isaac was a very smart engineer with a Ph.D. in electrical engineering. I, unfortunately, was no match for him. We would routinely get together to discuss his amazing inventions so I could draft patent applications.

The best time for Isaac to review these complicated technical matters was on Friday afternoons, just before we would both quit for the week. Isaac would visit my office around 3:00 p.m. and we would get started. Most of what he said went straight over my head. But he would begin to get thirsty and I would offer him a beer while I sipped iced tea.

After one beer, Isaac's brain downshifted a gear and I could at least follow what he was saying. After two beers, we were on an equal footing and I could ask intelligent questions.

One day, he was especially thirsty and accepted a third beer from me. That was a mistake. His I.Q. dropped so much, I was able to correct his equations. That's when I realized we had gone too far. I had more than leveled the playing field; I had tilted it in my favor. There was no point in being smarter than Isaac under the circumstances, so I resolved never to offer him three beers again.

Most recently, I was in a position to take a person down to my level not while performing an intellectual task like playing chess or understanding a Laplacian feedback electronic motor controller, but accomplishing a purely physical activity.

I have a friend named Alan who is quite an athlete. In high school he was captain of the swimming team. I once invited him to the swimming pool at my college and he easily broke the pool record for the breast stroke, back stroke, butterfly stroke, and freestyle for 200, 400, and 800 meters.

That's the sort of athlete Alan is -- one step away from being chosen for the Olympic swimming team, to hear him tell it.

I now live in Colorado and I snow ski at ski areas that are 10,000 feet above sea level, where the air is relatively thin. Alan, on the other hand, has never skied before visiting me and he certainly isn't accustomed to the thin air of Colorado ski resorts.

The first day on a skiing trip, he was a mess. Between the comparative lack of oxygen and his unfamiliarity with skis, I could ski rings around him, and I did. Gleefully, I might add. But by the second day on the slopes, Alan had not only learned the basics, he was already skiing down trails I was afraid to try.

The point of all this is I've learned to appear to be smarter or sometimes more athletic by subterfuge, deception, and trickery. In my book, that's almost as good as being above average.

Life as a Pomegranate

The other day I had the surreal pleasure of speaking with a pomegranate. This may sound fantastic, but suspend your disbelief for a few minutes. After all, stranger things than talking pomegranates have happened — at least to me.

My new friend, the talking pomegranate, suggested I could call him Pomeroy.

"Bein' a pomegranate ain't as simple or as relaxing as you might expect," Pomeroy said. "Oh sure, I'm grown in warm climates. I soak up the sun like a 1950s movie star and, basically, I dig the weather of Persia. I'm one of those entities that don't object to climate change. I think you call them Republicans."

"Whoa," I said. "Don't get started with me."

"Well, dude," Pomeroy continued, "the more the climate heats up, the more you'll see of me and my relatives, right up till our planet is reduced to cinders. That's all I'm sayin'."

I changed the subject. "Isn't it true the rind of the pomegranate fruit and the bark of the tree can control diarrhea, dysentery, and intestinal parasites?" I asked. "Maybe the College of Gastroenterology should adopt a pomegranate as its mascot."

"Darned right," said Pomeroy. "You sound like you're speaking from experience. You probably know my fruit can also treat hemorrhoids, but slatherin' up hemorrhoids with pomegranate juice results in colorful underwear — a small price to pay for being able to ride a bicycle, don't ya think?"

"Agreed," I said, shifting uncomfortably in my chair. "I've heard you're also a powerful source of antioxidants."

"Believe it, bro," Pomeroy said, his color turning even a deeper red. "I'm the best. Most people wouldn't know an antioxidant from an oxymoron. Punicalagin compounds are the major components responsible for our antioxidant benefits and they're found only in us pomegranates. Beat that."

"I'll try to remember 'punicalagin' for Scrabble games."

"Whatever," Pomeroy said. "And while we're on the subject, not to brag, but just sayin': a glass of pomegranate juice has more antioxidants than red wine, green tea, blueberries, or cranberries. We not only lower cholesterol, but also lower blood pressure and we help melt atherosclerosis. We've even been linked to longevity, even immortality, according to some ancient Chinese witch doctors. Did I tell you when squeezed into eye drops, our juice can slow development of cataracts?"

"That would help explain your sense of superiority," I said under my breath.

"Hey, buddy, I've got a pretty tough skin, or haven't you noticed? Now that you can sit comfortably and see clearly, you might be interested to know we can even help firm up sagging breasts (heh heh). And speaking of a subject near and dear to our hearts and other organs, we might help prevent or combat prostate cancer and erectile dysfunction, which is especially valuable if you're going to be immortal. I mean, without sex, living forever would feel like a very long time."

"I can only imagine," I said.

"I don't think you can, sparky."

"It sounds like you have a pretty enviable life," I said. "So why are you acting like the toughest guy in the orchard?"

"I'll tell you, my fruit-talking twerp. The thing that really fries my rind is confusion with the lowly, boring, common apple. The Persians got it right. They believed Eve actually plucked a pomegranate — not an apple — from the tree of knowledge in the Garden of Eden. In fact, we pomegranates are sometimes known as Chinese apples. My scientific name, punica granatum, even comes from Medieval Latin pōmum 'apple' and grānātum 'seeded.'

"And even though Greeks break us open at wedding celebrations because we symbolize prosperity and, of course, fertility, life isn't all, well, peachy. My seeds are encased in arils or arials and I'm squished among hundreds of other seeds in my colony, man, while I ripen. Sometimes 1,400 seeds are pressed against each other in each 5" bulb. Sardines have nothing on pomegranate seeds. Can you imagine? Well, I guess you can, since you're about to cut me open and yank my seeds right out of my membranes."

I didn't want to interrupt Pomeroy. He was on a roll.

"When we're processed to make juice and to make liquid flavoring for alcoholic drinks," he continued, "we're pushed and flattened and squeezed mercilessly under unbearable pressure, until our arils rupture and burst open and our juice spurts out. It's a barbaric way to extract our essence, if you ask me; I thought that technique went out with ancient Egyptians' method of extracting brains of cadavers through their noses. That's called excerebration, by the way, chump. And I dare you to use that word in polite conversation."

I felt badly about splitting open the fruit, but by this time I was really hungry. The discussion with Pomeroy the proud pomegranate gave me a lot to... um... chew on.

Life's a Gamble

It may have been Albert Einstein and his amusing friends, hammering out the details of quantum mechanics at the beginning of the last century, who started us on a path of uncertainty. Werner Heisenberg developed the famous Uncertainty Principle to explain how the smallest elements in the universe are individually unpredictable, but if you analyze enough of them, you find that they — like a school of fish — follow statistical rules. You may not know exactly where one sub-atomic particle is located, but you can figure out the probability of its being at a definite location. Basically, those physicists changed the way things are now perceived. Instead of determining exact properties, they relied on probabilities. It still doesn't make sense for objects we deal with. I mean, most of us who see a baseball heading for our head will duck, because we know exactly where that ball is heading. But that's not the case with atomic particles.

Nevertheless, quantum mechanics changed our outlook, even if we're not smashing atoms into each other.

Let me show you how different things are now, for you and me, compared to 100 years ago.

I know myself pretty well (finally)! For example, I know I have an addictive personality. I'm the guy for whom Lay's potato chips came up with the slogan, "Bet you can't eat just one." And I don't stop at potato chips. Peanuts, cookies, and M&Ms all entice me like Sirens singing to Odysseus. My middle name is Binge.

With an addictive personality, I dare not engage in drugs, tobacco, or alcohol. The same goes for gambling —

especially gambling. If I were to approach a roulette wheel, my night wouldn't end until I lost my house.

Of course, I am not alone. Sometimes even the most disciplined among us cannot resist the urge to bet. In our society, opportunities to gamble are thrust at us from every direction, like General Custer in Las Vegas — not to mix a metaphor — surrounded by casinos owned by tribes of Native Americans.

An entire lucrative and reputable industry has developed based on our temperaments. It's called the insurance industry. What is insurance, if not a gamble? You bet that you will get sick or die before your insurance policy expires so that you or your next of kin can benefit from the policy. The higher the premiums, the more the potential payout or reward.

And have you rented a car lately? You are asked to bet on whether you will return to the car rental with an empty tank of gas. The gas is prepaid, so if you don't use it all, down to the last expensive drop, you pay for it anyway. Last year I was sure I could beat the odds by planning to use up a tank. But I soon discovered my hotel was too close to the airport. It was also downtown within walking distance of every place I wanted to visit. So, I paid an exorbitant fee for parking at the hotel for five days, never moving my rented car, and returned it with a full, paid up tank. The experience cost me $250 more than if I had merely taken a taxi — even a private limousine — to and from the airport. Speaking of cars, why do we plunk our change into parking meters? It's because we're betting that we'll receive a more expensive parking ticket if we don't. In other words, parking meters are merely stationary slot machines with no opportunity for a payout — unless you pack a baseball bat in your trunk.

Let's talk about something fundamental: heating my house. My oil fuel delivery company is playing a game similar to the rental car companies. I can pay for a year's worth of oil at the present price — lock it in, regardless of how the price of oil will change this year. The company is willing to gamble that oil prices will drop, so it will win at my expense.

Of course, I'm a sucker for that kind of bet — they call it option contracts on Wall Street — believing that the price of oil will never decrease. Just the sort of famous last words that General Custer might have uttered on his way to the Battle of Little Big Horn.

Here's another example of gambling that corporations can get away with: air flights. If I book early, the airplane ticket is usually less than if I wait till the last minute. So I'm forced to gamble that nothing will happen to change my plans. It's cheaper to buy non-refundable tickets, too, but I can buy flight insurance — there's that insurance again — in case I can't make the flight. They sell that sort of insurance for ocean cruises, too. Basically, for every trip, I'm one medium-sized kidney stone away from regretting that I didn't buy travel insurance.

Telephone plans can be as bad. You can prepay for a certain number of minutes every month and bet you won't go over. The only way to win that bet is to keep your phone n your file cabinet.

Major appliances all have optional extended warranties. When you purchase one of them, you're betting that your dishwasher, say, will break down and flood the kitchen before you say good-bye to your obnoxious relatives at the end of the Thanksgiving weekend.

Even our federal government has gotten into the act. The feds want me to bet that I will live only a short time longer, now that I reached the age of 62, in which case it would be best to claim social security benefits now, rather than at age 65. But if I live much beyond 65 — and I'm betting that I will — it's better to defer collecting payments until I reach my 65th birthday, so I will receive larger monthly checks. Once again, I'm forced to bet against my life expectancy.

Einstein and his buddies probably weren't thinking that the laws of chance were going to affect the average person's life like they do; but chances are, things will get even less certain for us in the future.

In fact, I would bet on it.

Lottery Scams

This may be my last Weekend Radio essay. It's not because I've had a falling-out with my friend Robert Conrad after all these years or because I'm long overdue for retirement.

No, it's because I just won a $3 million prize in a lump sum.

As you might know, I'm an inveterate lottery player. I know the odds of winning the lottery are somewhat less than the odds of becoming an Olympic figure skating champion when I don't own a pair of ice skates. But it feels so good to buy a Lotto ticket twice a week. I walk around with a ticket in my pocket, thinking I have a chance to win a hundred million dollars or so. It's certainly worth two bucks to have that feeling.

Anyway, as it turns out, I did win a lottery. It's called the Princess Diana Universal Promo and my email address was apparently attached to ticket number 13-2316-5086-477; with serial number A025-09. Pretty cool, huh? I just knew if I kept buying lottery tickets, my number would come up. And it has.

You may recall that Princess Diana, the Princess of Wales, died on August 31, 1997 due to a car accident in Paris while fleeing from paparazzi. I sort of remembered that even though it was about 20 years ago, but the announcement letter I received reminded me again. It was a very informative letter.

Now honestly, I don't remember buying a lottery ticket for that contest, but who am I to object? The material I received says it's the British Parliament that receives yearly royalties in furtherance of the objectives of some foundation that was provided by the late Princess Diana in her will.

My email was selected through a computer-generated ballot system drawn from companies or individuals from the Middle East, Australia, New Zealand, Asia, Europe and North America. If it were just the 300 million Americans I beat out, that would be pretty lucky, but being the winner from a pool of a few billion people makes me feel very special (in addition to very rich).

The foundation that selected me stated:

> At this juncture, we finally congratulate and welcome you into the happy union of the friends and well-wishers of late Princess Diana, a woman of distinction, who whether in good times and bad, she never lost her capacity to smile and laugh, nor to inspire others with her warmth and kindness.

I'm thinking that Prince Charles may not have always received Princess Di's warmth and kindness, but I don't want to quibble with the gift horse that's distributing her estate.

The letter also stated that I'll be charged for advanced fees to cover expenses associated with delivery of the big check. That's a reasonable request, I think. It must be expensive to mail the check to me all the way from London. I'll be happy to pay whatever those advanced fees turn out to be. The foundation also needs my full name and address, my telephone number, my date of birth, my occupation, my business address, and my marital status -- all necessary, I guess, to write the check.

The foundation cautioned me to keep my winning information confidential until my claim is processed and my money remitted to me, due to the mix up of some numbers and names, they said. But I decided to let my listeners know

now, before I received the funds, because I'm really excited and I wanted to warn everyone that I'll be taking an early retirement.

So, there you have it. This is good-bye for good. My dreams have come true and I'm sincerely sorry for all the mean-spirited comments I've made about everyone. Except my mother-in-law.

Lucky Dog

My pal Cashew the Chihuahua and I took a walk last night and, along the way, I thought of all the advantages she has over me. For starters, Cashew has no use for toilet paper, tissues, deodorants, toothpaste, or mouthwash. Cashew gets occasional baths, but not a daily shower. And she never uses hair spray or hand lotion.

When it comes to hands and feet, she doesn't need shoes and socks when we venture outside... or when we're inside, now that I think of it. She doesn't have to tie shoelaces or shine her shoes or buy new ones when holes appear in her worn soles. She doesn't have to maintain her wardrobe in case she's ever invited to a formal party.

And stress? She doesn't know the meaning of the word. She's never had a job, so she has no experience dealing with office politics or balancing a home budget.

She has shown absolutely no interest in saving for retirement. In fact, as far as I can tell, Cashew has no financial care in the world. She doesn't have to make car payments or pay the rent or make health insurance, life insurance, flood insurance, or car insurance premiums, or pay taxes or pay her telephone bill or pay her college tuition or her wedding expenses. She never has to make the minimum payment on a credit card. She can't even tell the difference between a one-dollar bill and a C-note.

Although Cashew enjoys riding in a car with her head out the window, she has never studied for a driver's license. She's never changed a tire or filled up with lead-free gas. She never has to remember to switch off her left turn signal a mile after making a turn. She'll never turn over her registration to a policeman after breezing through one of the speed traps in Morrison, Colorado.

School is really a joke for Cashew. She's never taken a trigonometry exam or pulled an all-nighter working on a term paper. She's never memorized the capital of every state or the Gettysburg Address.

Her attention span is limited. She can't remember even a half dozen telephone numbers, which wouldn't matter, since she doesn't know how to digit dial anyway.

She never gets embarrassed if someone points out her fly is open or she has tomato sauce on her white shirt or her suit coat is slightly ripped or her necktie doesn't match her slacks or her clothes are way out of style. Actually, she doesn't know the meaning of the word, "style." Bad breath doesn't seem to faze her, nor does body odor.

She can't check her email, update her Facebook account, or perform a Google search. In fact, she doesn't know how to turn on a computer and apparently couldn't care less.

Cashew doesn't have to buy food or decide what to order at restaurants. She doesn't have to calculate a reasonable tip for the waiter or the sommelier, to say nothing of risking embarrassment about choosing an inappropriate wine with duck l'orange.

Those are just some of the obligations she's able to duck merely because, by accident of birth, she was born into a particular species.

But Cashew has an irrational fear of thunder, which I don't share. When a lightning storm begins, even before I hear the first peel of thunder, Cashew takes off for a safe place in my house and her little body shakes and quivers with fright. Except for very large, aggressive dogs, that's about the only fear she has.

On the other hand, the list of things Cashew doesn't fear is impressive.

She doesn't fear being drafted into the army.

She doesn't fear tangling up Saran Wrap.

She doesn't fear her electricity being turned off when she doesn't pay her bill.

She doesn't fear rejection by some snooty social group.

She doesn't fear high cholesterol, hypertension, liver disease, high blood sugar, or even death.

She doesn't fear smoking recreational pot in a state that's not as enlightened as Colorado.

She doesn't fear running out of medication, printer ink, ice cream, or toilet paper.

And perhaps most importantly, she doesn't fear the terrible loss when someone close to her, like me, for example, disappears.

March of the Coffee Mugs

A cup of coffee upset my stomach half a century ago and I haven't had a drop since. So, it's clear that I'm not a coffee drinker. In fact, outside of New York City, I'm told I don't even pronounce the word correctly. COFFEE. In 1969, a friend suggested that I try some new-fangled concoction called decaffeinated, which might not result in such noisy stomach rumbles. But somehow, I haven't gotten around to trying that yet.

It's not that I hate the taste. In fact, coffee ice cream is my favorite flavor. I like coffee candy, too. I even enjoy coffee commercials on TV.

But like smoking, if I haven't already started the habit, it's probably a good idea not to begin it now. You know, more and more doctors are telling their patients to cut down on their coffee consumption, regardless of what ails them. My wife — perfect in every other way — is addicted to the stuff. If she doesn't get her full nine cups per day, she goes through withdrawal — blinding headaches, shaky hands, the works.

By the way, the average American coffee drinker drinks a little more than three cups per day. For comparison, the French writer Honoré de Balzac imbibed up to 50 cups of coffee per day, yet he once said, "Coffee only makes boring people even more boring." Anyway, he died of heart failure at the age of 51.

Caffeine is the most widely consumed drug in the world. It is a psychoactive, addictive drug and, short of intravenously, coffee is about the best way to consume the stuff.

Various studies have linked coffee to insomnia (of course), fibrocystic breast cancer, high blood pressure, cholesterol, esophageal reflux, cardiac arrhythmias, dyspepsia, heart disease, constipation and diarrhea — but not at the same time — gall stones, osteoporosis, premenstrual syndrome, low birth weight babies, and even epilepsy.

Even coffee mugs can pose a hazard. In 2007, Starbucks recalled over 160,000 of its mugs with plastic handles that might detach, spilling hot coffee on many of their erstwhile loyal customers. They were made in China. And a year later, Sears recalled almost 150,000 coffee makers that posed a fire hazard. In case you're keeping track, they were also made in China.

Speaking of mugs, for a guy who doesn't drink coffee, I sure have a world-class coffee mug collection. I must have 200 of them, and everyone has a message. I have at least two from every bank in town. Some of the mugs have outlasted the banks they advertised. I also have a few from insurance companies, radio stations, local rock bands, our local zoo, our local museum, our local sheriff, non-profit organizations from "Save the Coal Miners" to "Save Our Planet," and even a T-shirt company. Really, how silly is it for a T-shirt company to advertise on a coffee mug?

They're perfectly good mugs, as far as I can see — although I haven't used more than three of them — so it would pain me to throw them out, especially the "Save Our Planet" one.

I wonder why so many of them are made and given away? As aforementioned, coffee itself is not very good for us; but is it so toxic that the stuff wears a hole in coffee mugs?

Most Expensive Things

W henever the lottery jackpot reaches $100 million or so, like probably everyone else I start to think about what I would do with all that money, once my taxes are paid and every friend and relative in my life receives the millions of dollars they request or demand from me.

Let's say I end up with $10 million, free and clear. That's still approximately $10 million more spending cash than I have at the moment. To put it in perspective, it represents a dinner for my wife and me, not including tips, at a very nice restaurant every night of the week for the next 260 years. It's the sort of place I never go to unless my father is paying.

That's what $10 million could buy.

But I have to be more realistic. I could get bored with that sort of lifestyle within a decade or two. Let's say I still have 9 million bucks and some change left over.

If I were really intent on spending the money, I would visit some pricey websites, like most-expensive.com/billionaire-gifts. Here are a few items within my future budget:

• The Amour dog collar was described by Forbes as "the Bugatti of dog collars." This is the most expensive dog collar I've seen. It features 1,600 diamonds including a 7-carat centerpiece, set in white gold and the price is a reasonable $3.2 million. I'm a bit afraid the collar will go to my Chihuahua, Cashew's, head. Soon she'll be demanding better dog food, the spoiled little princess.

• The Victoria's Secret Fantasy bra is an 18-karat white and yellow gold bra featuring 3,400 precious stones including diamonds (142 carats worth), pearls, citrines — whatever those are — and aquamarines. It's just another reason I think it's a shame that bras are usually covered up.

All the stones in the Secret Fantasy bra have been set by hand. The bra itself took 500 hours to complete, and I'll bet some of those hours were spent searching the carpet for a few of the stones that fell off the jeweler's bench. At $2.5 million, it looks like I'll have to find a new girlfriend and hope my adoring wife doesn't find out. Maybe that's why they call it Victoria's Secret.

• A fellow named Roman Abramovich purchased a gigayacht for $485 million. The listing says it's a luxury vessel, but it looks like a battleship to me. Of course, I can't buy the boat, since it would exceed my measly lottery winnings, but I can rent it for a week for only $2 million. If I can bargain with Roman, I might be able to have it for five weeks for the price of four. That's how billionaires think, by the way. I wonder if I can afford all the Dramamine I'll need.

- Dolce & Gabbana's Sunglasses are touted as being the most expensive sunglasses in the world. I have to admit they look very cool, but I'll have to check if the $380,000 price tag includes bifocals. For more than a third of a million dollars, I'd also demand a carrying case. See how easy it is to think like a billionaire?

- The Patek Philippe Platinum World Time wristwatch showcases times in 24 different time zones in addition to the home time. I didn't know so many time zones existed. It could come in handy if my airplane crashes, I end up somewhere in the Pacific Ocean, and I don't want to miss the Jerry Springer Show. The watch has a platinum chassis and, says the listing, quality leather straps. For $4 million, the straps better be quality.

- Now that I've purchased a pair of sunglasses and wristwatch in my mind's eye, I think a fountain pen would be appropriate. I found the world's most expensive pen, the Fulgor Nocturnus by the famous pen-makers Tibaldi of Florence. This fountain pen sold for $8 million in a 2010 auction in Shanghai, China. The pen is decorated with 945 black diamonds and 123 rubies. With my luck, ink for the pen is probably separately priced.

• When you think about big price tags, you might think of expensive automobiles. But I'd like to make even a more significant statement to my neighbors. So I've got my eyes set on The Big Bud 747 tractor, built by Northern Manufacturing, which comes in at 50 tons and costs $1.13 million dollars. It's higher than a one-story building. Now wouldn't that look good in front of my house?

• It's probably not a bad idea to be more frugal or I'll run out of spending cash faster than you can spell "bankruptcy." No need to spend millions of dollars on products if I can get away with a fraction of that amount and still impress people. That's why I'm focusing on Gold Shoelaces by a Mr. Kennedy. For only $19,000, I can purchase a set of those gold shoelaces, which surely go with every pair of shoes and sneakers I own. The good news is only ten pairs of gold shoelaces will be produced, which I'm thinking is ten more than the market will stand, now that Liberace is no longer with us.

Mountain Pride

I've lived in a number of places and visited many others, but I've never seen residents with as much pride as those who live in Colorado. You don't see many companies in, say, New Mexico, with the words "New Mexico" in their name. But in Colorado it seems like every other business is called Colorado something. By my count, 228 companies in the Denver phone book use the word, Colorado in their names.

There's a Colorado Hair Company, a Colorado Bead Company, a Colorado Guitar Company, and Colorado Creative Cabinetry, which is as alliterative as Colorado Cut & Color.

It's hard to think of an alliterative business name in New Mexico. The only one I can think of is "New Mexico's Nude Mannequins," which exists only in my mind but which resulted in interesting photos in my Google search.

In Colorado, we also have Coolerado Company, an air conditioner manufacturer with a sense of humor, especially since everyone tells me you don't need an air conditioner if you live in the mountains. However, the same people told me it hardly ever rains in this state. Tell that to all those people who were forced into a Holiday Inn because their house was flooded a couple of years ago.

The medical field has a disproportionate number of businesses that include the name of the state in which they reside. They begin to sound like an organ of the month club. We have Colorado Ear Nose & Throat, Colorado Heart Clinic, Colorado Comprehensive Spine, Colorado Center for the Blind, Urology Center of Colorado, Colorado Podiatry Consultants, Colorado Arthritis Center, and Colorado Serum Company. In case you're dozing off, you can visit the Colorado Snoring and Sleep Apnea Center. Most importantly, for some of my friends, we have the Colorado Mental Health Institute.

We also have Best Colorado Meds, not to be confused with Colorado Cannabis Company. You knew I'd get around to legal marijuana, didn't you? MMD of Colorado stands for Marijuana Medical Dispensary. Amerimed of Colorado performs evaluations for pain relief through medical marijuana. You would think people in the pot business would be more creative with their company names. I think they should consider changing their brand of psychoactive cigarettes.

Banking institutions don't want to be left out, either. Around here they include Bank of Colorado, Colorado Business Bank, Colorado Credit Union, Colorado Lending Group, Colorado State Bank and Trust and the much shorter Colorado Trust. So you see, my new, adopted state has a wealth — pardon the expression — of proud bankers. With that many banks, why was it so difficult to get a mortgage?

For the car industry, we have the Colorado Automobile Dealers Association at the top, followed by Colorado Classic Cars, Colorado Cab Company, Colorado Car Company, and Colorado Car Care. Not to leave anyone out, our state also includes Colorado Car Tinting, Colorado Auto & Parts, Colorado Custom Cylinder Heads, and Colorado Car Interiors.

Colorado business owners are obviously delighted with, and proud of, their state, but their enthusiasm is nothing compared to that of fanatical Denver Bronco fans in the football season.

My First Puppy

I got my first puppy just before I turned 63. I've had many reasons and excuses for not having a dog before now. They range from fear to increased responsibility and back to fear. My parents never considered owning a pet as my sisters and I grew up. I remember one exception, though: a 25¢ circus turtle came in a flimsy cardboard box with a plastic lid. I called him Tommy the Turtle. He lasted a day and a half and then we had to unceremoniously flush Tommy's little lifeless carcass down the toilet.

So no, I was unaccustomed to real, sentient pets for my whole life.

But I met this wonderful woman recently who captured my heart and for whom I would do anything, including moving a thousand miles and cohabiting with her dog. Her dog is a female Chihuahua, barely seven pounds. It never barks and never bites, which were two pleasant surprises for me.

One of the first things I learned is not to refer to the dog as a dog or as "it," as in "I'm getting used to having it in the house."

"You have to call her by her name, honey," this adorable woman suggested. "And if you don't call her by name, at least use a personal pronoun. 'She' or 'her' is preferable to 'it.'"

Needless to say, that sort of adjustment doesn't occur overnight. It took me six weeks to refer to it as she. And another two weeks to call it by its given name, "Cashew." In the beginning, I have to admit, I wasn't particularly comfortable calling Cashew by name in public.

I had another problem with the dog, I mean Cashew: I caught her staring at me while I was engaged in various activities, like reading or speaking on the phone. I would wake from a nap sometimes and notice her face only inches from mine, studying me in silence. That's the sort of thing that can give a person the willies.

It was eerie, downright spooky, thinking that she was sizing me up, judging me; okay, even laughing at me. The feeling was exacerbated when I undressed in her presence. In fact, I never fully got over that uncomfortable feeling; so to this day I undress for bed in the bathroom.

I understood that having a pet carries with it a great deal of responsibility. The owner has to feed it and fill its water bowl diligently, and take it to the veterinarian in emergencies and to trim its toenails. And I knew from overhearing pet owners, that some sort of dog sitter or kennel is needed when an owner wants to leave home and go to a movie.

But I really hadn't considered the most time-consuming part of the experience: I must take Cashew for walks, sometimes even more than once a day.

As I mentioned, Cashew is a Chihuahua and Chihuahuas, I have grown to understand, are temperamentally fearful creatures. It must come naturally, I think, because they are so small. My Cashew is no exception. She is especially nervous when she senses thunderstorms or garbage trucks. Recently, her fear of thunder has progressed even to a fear of clouds in the distance. As for garbage trucks, I wonder what the odds are of a truck cruising by during the week, exactly when we decide it's time to take a stroll.

One of her favorite hiding places, when a garbage truck is within five blocks of our home, is under the bed. That requires finding the little darling and trying to coax her to come out. Sometimes I am less persuasive than others, so I must resort to crawling under the damn bed, invariably in my suit and tie, and imploring her in a falsetto. You get the picture. By now, we're both in a bad mood and neither of us really wants to venture out. But of course, the consequences of letting her bladder continue to fill all day long while I'm at my office make me shudder.

When I first met Cashew, she had a leash that fit snugly around her neck. I felt like a cruel master choking her to guide her where I wanted her to go. So I replaced the leash with a body harness and I feel so much better now — less a master and more a friend who occasionally has to gently crush her ribs when we take a walk.

Cashew has interesting — I might say endearing — mannerisms. She often approaches me on her rear legs and gently paws my leg to get my attention. The conversation that ensues is right out of a Lassie episode.

"What's the matter, Cashew?"

No answer. Pawing continues.

"Is Timmy in trouble?"

Silent pawing intensifies, like some weird game of Charades.

"Did he fall down the well again?"

Her pawing reaches a fever pitch, and I realize she doesn't understand a word I'm saying. I don't know a Timmy and I don't have a well. Sarcasm is totally lost on Cashew. Likewise, her urgent desire to communicate sometimes doesn't make sense to me, either.

So, I ignore her and she soon gets involved in some other activity that doesn't require my participation, like shredding my Sunday newspaper.

When she's happy, she gets excited and commences to chase her tail in ever-smaller, counterclockwise circles. Her revolutions can reach 240 r.p.m. for short bursts of time, which causes at least one of us to get dizzy.

When does she get that excited? When I happen to mention that I'll give her a doggie treat. "Treat" is one of the three words she knows. She gets so excited when I merely rattle a plastic bag that contains said treats, or even when I approach the kitchen.

It's taken a while, but my dog finally has me trained. And darned if I don't like her enough now to call her Cashew. Even in public.

My Friend, the Pine Tree

I've become very fond of a ponderosa pine tree on my property. It would be presumptuous to call this independent organism "my tree," because such marvels of nature cannot be possessed.

In 1913, Joyce Kilmer wrote a poem. Joyce, by the way, was a man and his full name was Alfred Joyce Kilmer. He was killed by a sniper's bullet five years later during the First World War at the age of 31. Here's part of his poem:

> I think that I shall never see
> A poem lovely as a tree.
> Poems are made by fools like me,
> But only God can make a tree.

That about sums it up for all of us, doesn't it?

This pine tree out my living room window is about 50 feet high. The window is a big picture window, so I can see the entire tree.

The tree could be more than 100 years old now. It must have started growing before I was born and will no doubt still be here after I'm gone. So right off the bat, I'm humbled by both its size and its age.

A few of its lowest limbs have been amputated over the years –- I almost said, "truncated" -- and the upper branches are curved in an S-shape, but the tree stands proudly, majestically against the Colorado sky. For those of you who haven't been in Colorado, a Colorado sky is a deep blue with absolutely no clouds. It's hard to describe without reference to a PMS paint color chart. It's about a PMS number 294, if you want to look that up.

The tree has been through countless wind, rain, ice storms, and blizzards. When the wind blows, the tree's limbs sway and the pine needles quiver. And when it snows here -- often measured in feet, not inches -- the tree stoically remains steadfast against the onslaught, each branch supporting an impossible quantity of snow. It knows that any temporary inconvenience will pass, as it has for dozens of years.

It's that indifference that also humbles me. Anything short of a forest fire or a chainsaw will not perturb the tree's serenity.

The trunk of the tree is offset from neighboring trees, of which there are many in my backyard. Some of the branches of the tree touch branches of neighboring trees. That must give the tree comfort, diminishing the loneliness it has to feel most of the time.

At certain times in the late spring and summer, thousands of pinecones fall from its branches, littering the forest floor. The tree is fecund during those times, hoping that at least some of the pinecones will find root and carry on the DNA of the tree to future generations. It will likely never see its progeny, but it can live in hope every year that its children will flourish.

That is a fair description of the tree, its thoughts and feelings, but here's what the tree can't do. It can't move from its location – the location it has occupied for perhaps 200 years. It also can't ride in a car, train, or airplane. It cannot see or hear television programs or attend concerts or root for a baseball team. It can't experience great literature. It can't take advantage of clothing or furniture or automobile sales. It can't celebrate any occasion, taste birthday cake or exotic flavors of ice cream. It can't bundle up before a roaring fire on a cold night.

It can't engage in a stimulating conversation with its relatives and friends on Thanksgiving Day. And it can't taste a turkey or sweet potato pie.

It can't take a vacation to a distant land or take photographs of people, places, and things.

But despite those shortcomings, it can experience tranquility, solitude, and patience better than any of us can. So you see, a fool like me envies the tree that stands outside my window and the joys it feels.

My Idols are Mostly Dead

One of the unanticipated consequences of growing older, for me, is discovering that I have outlived the people I used to admire. I suppose that's inevitable if I live long enough, but it was a revelation to me. For example, the actor George C. Scott is dead. Can you mention General Patton without seeing George C. Scott in front of that giant American flag? That's not to say there aren't great stage, TV, and movie actors who are performing now, but I enjoyed just about every George C. Scott performance. I can still hear his raspy voice. And who but Paul Newman could be Hud?

Film directors, too, have fallen from the ranks: Alfred Hitchcock and John Huston and Stanley Kubrick and Orson Welles are all gone.

I miss Beverly Sills' operatic performances, even though she had not performed seriously for years before she passed away. It saddens me, though, just knowing that she will never sing again. Classical conductors Leinsdorf, Ormandy, Bernstein, and Steinberg will never again wield their batons, but at least some of their recordings live on on CDs or scratchy vinyl.

Isaac Stern will never play what he called his fiddle again and Marcel Marceau will never mime again.

On the popular song front, I'm not the only one who misses Elvis, Ritchie Valens, Dean Martin, and the chairman of the board; but the fact that others miss them too doesn't make me feel any better.

276

Professional sports haven't been the same once we lost Micky Mantle, Joe DiMaggio, Johnny Unitas, and Dale Earnhardt.

I no longer peruse bookstore shelves for new novels by Arthur C. Clarke, Charles Harness, and Isaac Asimov. Asimov wrote some 450 books. I never thought the flood of his books would end, but suddenly they did.

A web site lists celebrities, their date of birth, whether they are still alive and, if not, their date and cause of death. The site is deadoraliveinfo.com. Causes of death range from diseases to old age to — in the case of Sonny Bono's skiing accident — a tree. At first, I was fascinated with the list of the living and the dead, but I haven't visited the deadoraliveinfo site lately. It depresses me.

Nothing depresses me as much as finding that a comedian or comic actor — often younger than I am — is dead. I expected that we'd lose Groucho Marx, Red Skelton, Sid Caesar, Bob Hope, Lucille Ball, Jack Benny, and even George Carlin, but why Freddie Prinze, John Belushi, and Chris Farley, all before the age of 35? The amazing comedic genius, Robin Williams, is no longer spewing humor faster than most of us can absorb it, so I won't be smiling, if not laughing my head off, with him again.

On a happier note, Pacino and De Niro are still with us, as are the incredibly versatile Dustin Hoffman and Meryl Streep. More phenomenal performances are anxiously awaited. I wish we could see more of the remarkable Michael Keaton. His facial expressions illustrate exactly what he's thinking like no other actor. Life goes on and I still have the songs and movies and books to refresh the memory of those who checked out before the rest of us.

Naming Your Dog

One of the most important responsibilities for a new dog owner is naming his dog. Just like a person, a dog will grow into its name. If you name your son, "Buster," he's likely to become a bully or a professional rugby player or both. I'm not saying no Busters are in touch with their feminine side, but I haven't yet met a flower arranger named Buster.

Similarly, a daughter named "Priscilla" is not apt to become a rollerblade team captain or a long-haul hazardous material truck driver. In my experience, Priscillas excel at cookie baking and scarf knitting, not prize fighting.

But back to naming your dog.

Common dog names result in boring dog behaviors. So, don't even think of "Spot" or "Sparky" or "Rover" if your new dog has any personality at all.

On the other hand, you don't want to burden your dog with an appellation that will subject him to ridicule, like "Reginald" or "Horatio." Names like that will be an invitation for the other neighborhood dogs to victimize him.

Besides, giving your dog a human name will have a tendency to convince him he's human. Before you know it, he's sitting at your dining room table sharing your lasagna, to say nothing of your Beaujolais. He's also demanding a four-paw pedicure and giving you a disdainful look when you reach for the nail clippers.

While researching this topic in depth, I learned women often have a soft spot for dogs, especially adorable little puppies. In the words of my bachelor friends, dogs are chick magnets.

I've given this topic some thought, as you can see. So, it shouldn't surprise you to learn I'm all set with the perfect name, in case I actually acquire a dog someday. I won't keep you in suspense. I'm going to call my new dog, "I Love You."

One of the beauties of that name is it can be used for both genders.

What could be more adorable for a young woman than a puppy named, "I Love You?" I can just imagine the positive reaction I'll get when I whisper "Come here, I Love You," or maybe even, "Don't pee there, I Love You." When things are going well, of course, I might say, "Good girl, I Love You." When I'm frustrated, though, I might explode, "Darn it, I Love You, get out of the garbage."

This is actually one of my better ideas, so you can glean the quality of my other ones.

All I have to do now is find a puppy that can live up to its name. There has to be one for me. Where are you, I Love You?

Note to My Descendants

Hi there. This is Mark Levy from way back in the early days of the 21st century. I understand that you're listening to this 500 years from when I wrote it, long enough to be interested in how we used to live, but not so long that flight attendants have stopped educating you on proper seatbelt operation.

Speaking of air travel, we in America are now required to remove our footwear before being allowed to approach aircraft. I guess 500 years from now, before enduring your plane ride, you must be pretty much naked.

Let me describe things that already seem primitive. They're sure to give you a chuckle. For example, certain business people are required to wear long, snake-like apparel tied around their neck, if you can believe it, when they leave their homes to go to their office every morning, Mondays through Thursdays and sometimes Fridays.

Women are still treated differently from men. Most don't have to wear these elongated fabrics around their necks, but a lot of them have been convinced to overpay for articles that hold their tissues, keys, and sunglasses. These things are portable and have handles as well as names permanently affixed to them. No, not the women's names, but the manufacturers' names of these so-called bags, clutches, purses, or pocketbooks. Ditto for the sunglasses. Oh, those names of others also appear on shirts, pants, running shoes, and wristwatches.

In some circles, if you don't have the right name on the right articles, you are not permitted to fraternize with people who do. I'm sure that that silly fad hasn't survived the centuries.

We have something called salad bars for mass feeding. These are generally long food serving stations in which semi-warm, semi-stale foodstuffs are presented to people who are willing to risk their health to save money. For one price the greater their health risk, so the less they pay per pound.

Many of us these days aren't overly concerned about our health. We believe that medical science will come to our rescue, once we figure out how to pay for it, to cure obesity, ulcers, heart disease, kidney disease, liver disease — doesn't this sound like a sickly organ of the month club? —cancer, diabetes, stress, MS, MD, CF, CP, Parkinson's, Alzheimer's, irritable bowel syndrome, gall stones, and the common cold. Okay, maybe I'm exaggerating about the common cold, but I was on a roll.

We do believe we're only a pill away from curing the rest of our ailments. I'll bet you people living in 2500 A.D. don't have a health care in the world. You're probably in the place our grandparents believed we'd be in now when they were making predictions in 1950.

Speaking of predictions, no, we still haven't established colonies on the moon yet. Our life expectancy hasn't even reached 100, much less 300 and our gas mileage is about the same as when Henry Ford rolled out his first Model A. But now, thanks to GPS systems, we know where we are when we run out of gas and we can listen to satellite radio while we wait for the tow truck.

I wish I knew if male pattern baldness would still be with us in 500 years. It's the sort of thing that keeps me up at night.

Oh, Those Commercials

The number of television commercials seems to increase every time I turn on my T.V. set. Maybe if broadcasters would charge more for sponsors' time, I wouldn't have to spend so much prime time viewing medications for treating diseases I never heard of. But then again, the sponsors would pass on the expense to us consumers by increasing the prices of their products. Some days you just can't win.

Perhaps the proliferation of commercials is due to the fact that they aren't limited to one minute or 30 seconds anymore. We're down to 15-second spots, which means I can be subjected to a dozen ads in just three long minutes. I hate to give sponsors and T.V. executives another suggestion, but why limit the time slot for each commercial to only 15, 30, or 60 seconds? Why not splatter us viewers with 5 or 3 or 2 second spots? That way we can be exposed to dozens of messages every minute.

I'm intrigued when I see the exact same ad twice during one commercial break. That almost instant déjà vu makes me doubt my sanity, like I need another excuse to do that.

Sometimes different competing products are advertised, one after the other. Pepsi and Coke come to mind, as do Chevys and Fords. I guess that's handy for comparison shoppers, but they can be annoying to people like me who are indecisive in the first place, and just want to get back to reruns of The Big Bang Theory.

In order to do something other than gorge on popcorn between shows, I've started to focus on what most of us ignore. For example, now I keep track of the commercials. I recently counted 14 ads in a single commercial break. I'm hoping to set a new record soon. And of the 14 ads, guess how many I was able to recall a minute after the barrage? I'm not sure, but I think I remember one of the ads featured a little boy driving his father's car. I remember thinking that was a cute ad, but darned if I can identify the car if I see it on the road now, unless I happen to see the kid driving it.

Unfortunately for advertisers, the most effective commercials are least clever. Truly creative commercials may be more enjoyable for the viewer, but their message is overwhelmed by their very creativity. The example I just gave of the little boy driving his father's car is only one instance of the product being forgotten when the ad is too clever for its own good.

Here are a few others that come to mind. See if you can think of the product being sold when an actor said, "Where's the beef?" or "I can't believe I ate the whole thing," or "Stronger than dirt." There's also, "Quality never goes out of style" and "When there is no tomorrow" and "Think small."

I'm just glad I don't have to come up with ideas for commercials. It's all I can do to remember to turn off the T.V. set before I fall asleep.

Ordinary People with Famous Names

In Denver, a woman named Amelia Earhart used to report on traffic from a helicopter for a local news station. The broadcast news people at that Denver TV station didn't crack a smile when they introduced Amelia Earhart in her helicopter. Maybe they were all born too late.

This got me thinking about famous names in unlikely places. With the help of an Internet search engine that uses U.S. census data to arrive at its statistics, I discovered that there are more than 79,000 Amelias and almost 3,000 Earharts, but only one Amelia Earhart in America. Apparently, she's the one flying around in a helicopter. And how many of the three Charles Lindberghs even have pilot licenses?

It must be difficult to go through life with a famous person's name. People either expect too much of you or don't take you seriously. If you're one of the three Frank Sinatras, for example, you probably have to be ready to sing a few bars of My Way at the drop of a fedora.

Have any other of the two Mickey Rooneys or the 4,400 Elizabeth Taylors been married eight times?

Of all the 18,000 Lincolns in America, how many would you guess are Abrahams? The Internet says only three.

Are all the 342 Bob Hopes funny?

You may not know that more than 500 people are named Roy Rogers, yet there are only 429 Dale Evans to go around, making for almost 100 lonesome cowboys.

There are estimated to be 19 William Shakespeares, but nary a Hamlet in sight, prince or otherwise.

Here's another interesting statistic: only 276 people are named Jaclyn Smith, which just doesn't seem like enough.

If you'd like to check the frequency of your name or someone else's, visit the web site. HowManyOfMe.com.

People Born the Same Year as You

I recently found a fascinating website, one that kept me occupied for much too much time when I should have been doing something productive, like sorting M&Ms. But I guess that's what weekends are for, right? What did people do to entertain themselves before the Internet was invented? I'll have to google that sometime.

The web site that I discovered is called FamousBirthdays.com. You can plug in the year you were born and you will see photos of all the famous people born that year. When you click on a photograph, you will see the person's birthday, place of birth, occupation, marriage partner or partners, rank in popularity, and other riveting trivia.

Of course, if you are as vain as I am, you will start with your own birth year, but then you'll start to browse other years and before you know it, you'll realize you missed breakfast, lunch, and Weekend Radio.

So, let's start with the year I was born and see if anyone born that year is more famous than I am. The year was 1948. (I know, I don't sound that old.)

Now 1948 was a great year to be born if you're a musician. I share that birth year with singers Ozzie Osbourne, Olivia Newton-John, Steven Tyler, Robert Plant, Alice Cooper, Lulu, Stevie Nicks, Grace Jones, Rick James, James Taylor, Donna Summer, Kenny Loggins, Cat Stevens, composer Andrew Lloyd Webber, pianist Jessica Williams, drummer John Bonham, and guitarists Ted Nugent, Glenn

Frey, and Toni Iommi. See? I'm in good company, even if I can't carry a tune.

A number of actors were born my year, also. FamousBirthdays.com mentions Samuel L. Jackson, Billy Crystal, Kathy Bates, John Ritter, Carl Weathers, Phylicia Rashad, Avery Brooks, Bernadette Peters, Rhea Perlman, Pam Ferris, Jeremy Irons, Lewis Black, and Si Robertson... you know, from Duck Dynasty. All of those people seem older than I am, which makes me feel pretty good, even if I'm not that famous.

In sports, hockey player Bobby Orr, Terry Bradshaw, and Ray Misterio, the wrestler, share my 1948 birth year. Speaking of wrestling, Linda McMahon, who developed World Wrestling Entertainment, is also a 1948 baby. I can't help mentioning that Richard Simmons is the only fitness guru listed for my year.

Politicians born in 1948 include Al Gore and Prince Charles, who is the longest-serving heir apparent in British history and the oldest heir apparent in 300 years. I'm sharing that bit of trivia to give you the gist of the sort of information you can find on the FamousBirthdays.com site.

George R.R. Martin is the only author listed, which I found hard to believe. So I appear to be unique as a radio essayist born that year.

I can't help thinking what a loss to our country it would be if 1948 never existed.

If you were also born in 1948, there's no need for you to check out the FamousBirthdays.com website, since I've just told you all the good parts. But chances are, you were born in some other year. Don't miss the opportunity to see who else shares your birth year. It's sure to keep you occupied for more time than you want to spend.

I was curious to see who else was born the year Robert Conrad appeared, but FamousBirthdays doesn't go back that far.

Playing Hooky from Golf

Isn't it just wonderful to get outside on a golf course on a nice, sunny day to enjoy the weather, the scenery, and the tranquility of nature?

Golf courses are well kept and the greens are immaculate, a deep shade of green that you would think couldn't possibly occur in nature. The grass is cut uniformly, each blade being the same height as all the rest of the blades within a quarter of an inch. I can't shave my face with the same consistency. It's really a flawless achievement of manicuring.

The experience for most golfers ranges from sublimely relaxing to memorable. Even when the golfer doesn't win his or her game, the experience is unbeatable. I can see why the game is an obsession for so many people.

Unfortunately, I am not one of them.

I've visited driving ranges half a dozen times and I've been on golf courses a few times, but no matter how much I practice, I never get better at this game. My performance is sporadic at best, scoring in three digits before I stop counting my strokes. I can hit a ball solidly once in a while, but that shot is followed by a series of botched strokes creating massive divots on the very rare occasions when I don't miss the ball entirely. I think golfers call that whiffing.

One of my friends observed what he believed to be my problem. "Mark," he said, "I know what you're doing wrong."

Of course, he got my attention, as he was watching me hack away for a number of holes, racking up an impressive total of triple bogeys.

"You're standing too close to the ball," he said, "... after you hit it."

Typically, I improve, even slightly, when I continue to perform most activities, athletic or not, from skiing to tennis to writing. The more I practice, the better I get. Most people are like that. It's the way life is supposed to be. But for me golf is different. I don't seem to get better at it no matter how much I practice. The game loses its spontaneity when I have to remember how to stand, how to hold my head, my arms, and my hips, how to hold the club, how to aim down the fairway, how to swing, and how to follow through with my swing, to say nothing of having to remember how many strokes I took when I eventually get to the cup.

One rainy Sunday I had an opportunity to analyze my ambivalent feelings about the sport. It turns out the most enjoyable part of playing golf for me is not actually hitting or attempting to hit the ball. The best part is riding around in those nifty electric golf carts. They don't even have a brake pedal. They go when you step on the accelerator and they stop quickly when you remove your foot. They run on a silent electric motor and coast along the flats and inclines effortlessly, like floating above the land.

I just love that. I get to experience the pleasant weather and the scenery, feel a slight breeze, enjoy the freedom of mobility, and absorb the serenity of the experience without the frustration of actually trying to hit a ball that takes me ten minutes to find in the woods. I even look forward to having a well-deserved beer at the end of the exercise. Yes, navigating down the course in my rented cart is just about a perfect pastime.

So recently I decided to try to replicate the best part of my golf game without visiting a golf course. I applied for a job with a small landscape gardening company that maintains the area's adjacent roadways. These guys use golf carts to zip around the grounds they're responsible for. You can see them on the side of the road sometimes as you whiz by in your car.

The first day on the job, I was assigned my own golf cart with instructions to retrieve objects that could pose an obstacle to heavy lawn-cutting equipment, things like branches, rocks, and, of course, beer cans. I was told to expect a promotion to an industrial lawnmower someday if I executed my duties responsibly.

I thought things were going very well that first day so I decided to take a break in my tasks after a big lunch. I pulled over under a large tree, planning to close my eyes for just a few minutes. There's nothing like the soft breeze of a summer's day to relax a tired worker. The afternoon was punctuated with soft buzzing and humming of assorted flying insects in the distance. All in all, this was turning into a lovely day.

I guess my few minutes of relaxation somehow turned into a longer period, because I was awakened abruptly by my supervisor smashing into my golf cart with his. He apparently didn't appreciate the more subtle pleasures of being outdoors and communing with the aforesaid flying insects. We had words to that effect. And then he fired me.

I rented a golf cart from my local golf course last week. I even asked for a discount. I told the person renting the cart that I wouldn't be using the bag rack of the cart. After all, there's no point in lugging a golf bag around in it. Oh, and if I decide to slip into a gentle sleep under a tree, there's a good chance no one will bother me.

Playing with Matches

It's not easy living to the ripe old age of two thousand five hundred years, especially if you're a sequoia tree protected by park rangers in a national park. I visited Yosemite National Park recently and was appalled to see so many trees in the Mariposa Grove burned to the ground. The National Park Service, or NPS, has decided that the best way to prevent catastrophic fires is to remove the fuel by, well, by burning it.

Now these were the same folks who, 20 years ago, realized that the devastating fires in Yellowstone occurred because the rangers had a policy of dowsing fires wherever they could. That had been their policy for almost 100 years. But someone admitted the error of their ways. The policy was changed after 1988 to allow fires to burn themselves out, so there would be less chance of overly-dense foliage contributing to runaway fires. So far, so good. The National Park Service admitted a mistake and corrected it.

Now I'm afraid the NPS has over-compensated. Instead of waiting patiently for fires and opportunities to ignore them, the NPS is taking affirmative steps to prevent natural fires by burning up trees — living and dead. What a brilliant approach!

I have only a few concerns:

The NPS has been wrong before, if you remember.

The smoke from the rangers' fires is a health hazard to animals and humans. When I clawed my way to the top of Sentinel Mountain, wheezing and gasping, I could barely appreciate the view of Half-Dome and El Capitán, as they were almost entirely obscured by smoke.

As Albert Einstein once said, "I'm no Einstein," but it seems to me that people visit national parks, at least in part, to get away from the pollution in cities and towns. It's quite a nasty surprise to find more smoke in what is supposed to be a pristine park than in a bar-b-q ribs contest.

Assuming global warming is a fact and our civilization is partly to blame, should one of our most environmentally-aware organizations be burning tons and tons of wood every year?

If the goal is to remove potential firewood — and as you can see, I'm not convinced that's a logical goal, given the NPS's recent track record — why not cut the trees and sell them to lumber mills? Maybe the profit could be applied to road construction crews, so they could delay more cars of visitors. But that's a topic for another day.

Here's another concern: when the National Park Service says it's controlling a fire, who can really believe that? Would anyone be surprised to learn that a few extra thousand acres of woodland were accidentally destroyed due to the bumbling efforts of the well-intentioned fire brigade?

And here's my last concern:

What if this hare-brained scheme of the NPS is flat wrong, like the policy it abandoned 20 years ago? Are we willing to wait a few thousand years for nature to re-grow giant redwoods and sequoias?

Presidential Currency

I was sorting through my vast trove of cash the other day, well my one-dollar bills, actually, placing them face up in serial number order as I like to do. And it occurred to me that the face of all U.S. currency has much in common. They all have engravings of famous Americans, mostly presidents and, of course, and Ben Franklin on the biggest denomination, the one-hundred-dollar bill. All of the bills are printed with green ink.

It struck me that the price of just about everything has increased over the years. Chewing gum that used to cost a penny can only be bought in plastic containers now for a buck or more. My new car cost more than my first house.

There are fewer and fewer items that can be purchased for less than $100. We used to have a $500 bill. That would now be worth less, in real terms, than a $100 bill was worth in 1969.

What we need is a bigger denomination than the one-hundred-dollar bill. We used to have a one-thousand-dollar bill, which sported the likeness of Grover Cleveland on its face. High-denomination bills were last printed on December 27, 1945. But the Federal Reserve System decided to discontinue issuing thousand dollar bills in 1969, due to 'lack of use'.

Frankly, I think we should bring the thousand-dollar bill back and I know just the president who would be appropriate for its face. Someone who embodies wealth, financial success, and over-the-top self-worth.

The Treasury Department will have to stop using green ink, since those bills will be more lifelike in orange.

R.C. is a Popular Handle

The other day I was thinking about Robert Conrad, the debonair host of this show, and it occurred to me that his initials, R.C., might be used as shorthand in a number of fields. So, I searched the Internet for abbreviations and acronyms and found a web site called AcronymFinder.com. According to that site, the letters R.C. are used as an abbreviation 167 times to refer to everything from Race Car to Red Cross to Rear Commodore, whatever that is. The letters R.C. are also used as an acronym 241 times.

Considering how long Robert Conrad has been on the radio, I guess it's not surprising to find radio and electrical engineering terms that appropriate his initials. For example, R.C. can mean Remote Control, Remote Component, Radio Controlled, Radio Check, Radio Canada, Radio Catalunya, Radio Casablanca, Resistor-Capacitor circuit, Rated Current, Receiver, Record Changer, Records Custodian, and non-directional radio transmitter beacon. Frankly, I haven't figured out where the "C" shows up in that one.

The letters R.C. are used by at least a dozen institutions of higher learning and Research Centers — oops, that's another one; everything from Robert College in Istanbul to the famous Rutherford College in New Zealand.

Some other famous people share Robert Conrad's initials. There's the singer/performer Ray Charles, the baseball pitcher, Roger Clemens, the actor Russell Crowe, and the soon-to-be famous band, Redeye Carl — spelled with a "C" — & the Pirates. Wouldn't it be a kick to have all of them show up at, say, Rockefeller Center some day? It would be a sort of celebrity Rainbow Coalition.

With a small change in his accent and perhaps a shift in his temperament, I can see Robert Conrad turn into a Ragin' Cajun. After all, there's a Ragin' Cajun rollercoaster, known as the R.C. But no matter how drastic his personality may change, the Ragin' Cajun still won't have to change the initials on his luggage.

After this extensive research, I'll find it difficult to hear the dulcet sounds of Robert Conrad's voice without immediately associating him with the unfortunate adjectival phrase, Reduced Capacity.

Simplicity

The story is, Albert Einstein showed up at breakfast one day with a number of small nicks and cuts on his face.

"Herr Professor," his colleague said, "why are you so bruised?"

"From shaving," Einstein replied.

"What shaving soap do you use?"

"The same one I use for my hands and body."

"Ach. That is the problem. You should use shaving soap for your face."

"You mean," Einstein said, "there's a separate soap for shaving? Much too complicated."

Now I'm not saying I deserve to be compared to the smartest guy in the last century, but apparently, we have at least one common trait: a desire for simplicity.

For example, speaking of soap, you know that liquid hand soap people use in their bathroom and shower? I don't like it. I prefer the old-fashioned bar of soap... and not the new-fangled huckleberry scented ones or the ones that smell funky, like asparagus and salsa. No, the 99 and 44/100^{ths} pure soap is good enough for me.

When I stay in a motel, I refuse to use the hand towel and the bath towel. One is enough. If I can dry my whole body with a bath towel, it usually has enough capacity to dry my hands, too — both of them.

I like my pizza plain, just cheese and pizza sauce: no pepperoni, no pineapple, and hold the anchovies, just like when I was a teenager 50 years ago. Of course, the price of a slice of pizza has increased about 2,000% since then. I guess we all have to subsidize anchovies nowadays. In Colorado, people who have eaten the tasty part of their pizza slice pour honey on the outer crust, which, I have to admit, is a nice idea, and not too complicated. Try it yourself.

When it comes to the 800 television channels on cable, I ignore just about all of them. I still watch The Today Show most mornings. There's no need to check in with the new-fangled Good Morning America team. CNN World News looks like a short-lived fad to me. Who really needs that much breaking news every day?

Have you seen what they've done to Pringles potato chips? In addition to the original, potato chip-flavored product, you can now buy Pringles in these flavors: BBQ (barbecue), Xtra Fiery Sweet BBQ, Memphis Barbeque, Honey Mustard, Honey Mustard BBQ, Cheddar Cheese, French Onion Dip, Sour Cream and Onion, Buffalo Ranch, Pizza Flavor, Bacon and Pizza Flavor, Ninja Pizza, Tortillas Truly Original, Tortillas Nacho Cheese, Tortillas

Southwestern Ranch, Tortillas Zesty Salsa, Screamin' Dill Pickle, and Xtra Tangy Buffalo Wing.

I'm saving up to buy all of them for a Fourth of July taste test with 35 of my closest friends.

And it's not just Pringles that has flooded the market with so many new flavors. No, almost every product now has enhanced variations on the original flavor. Halfway through the arduous elimination process on the food aisle, I sometimes forget what I'm looking for. But it takes only the memory of one can of Screamin' Dill Pickle Pringles to remind me to refocus on the labels.

Stamphood

I I want to be famous. And it's not just because I want people to ask for my autograph or a selfie as I walk down the street or because I want to be listed in history books or because I want to be rich. Yes, of course I want all those things, but the main reason I want to be famous is so my face can be on an official U.S. postage stamp. Wouldn't it be great to achieve immortality by being recognized by those dozens of people who don't use email yet?

Here's the good news: it's easier to get your picture on a stamp than ever before. It used to be you had to be a former president or a famous person who was dead ten years. But in 2007, the U.S. Postal Service changed its policy so people had to be deceased only five years before they were eligible for the honor of appearing on a stamp. As of 2012, though, even living Americans can now be eligible for stamphood.

The first stamp of the U.S. was offered for sale on July 1, 1847. The stamp issue was really two stamps: an engraved 5-cent red brown stamp depicting Benjamin Franklin, the first postmaster of the U.S. in 1775, and a 10-cent stamp with George Washington's face on it. The more expensive stamp was for letters that were intended to travel 300 miles or more to their destination. If you find either one, unused, in very fine condition, you can sell it for $6,000 and $28,000, respectively.

No one thought about perforating the stamps until ten years later. Before perforations, people had to cut the stamps and affix them to their envelopes. It must have been a satisfying process for letter writers. It would give them a feeling of contributing to the delivery process, sort of meeting the Post Office half way.

The American flag did not appear on U.S. postage stamp issues until the Battle of White Plains Issue was released in 1926. Law makers were concerned that canceling stamps with an image of the flag could be considered desecration of the flag. The first U.S. postage stamp to feature the flag as the sole subject wasn't issued until July 4, 1957.

Over the years since 1847, more than 4,000 stamps have been issued and over 800 people have been featured. Some of these people have been featured on multiple stamps. As you would expect, featured on postage stamps are politicians, artists, authors, musicians, composers, singers, movie stars, scientists, architects, sports figures, photographers, and business leaders. So are astronauts and Supreme Court justices.

President Franklin D. Roosevelt did a lot fo philatelists, sic he was one himself. He had a collection of one million stamps. May designs of stamps in the 1930s were conceived or refined by Roosevelt while he was president.

In 1976, for the 200th anniversary of the Declaration of Independence, a whole slew of Declaration signers all got their own stamps. I had forgotten there were so many.

I was interested to find that many comedians have been honored by postage stamps. For example, Jack Benny, Milton Berle, Fanny Brice, W.C. Fields, Jackie Gleason, Groucho Marx, Will Rogers, Red Skelton, and Phil Silvers all have stamps. Good for them. They all deserve the honor. Comedic couples are represented by Bud Abbott & Lou Costello, George Burns & Gracie Allen, and Stan Laurel & Oliver Hardy. The Three Stooges, incredibly, have been overlooked.

I could find only one lawyer, believe it or not, who wasn't a Supreme Court justice or a president or a Declaration of Independence signer. His name is John Robert ("J.R.") Clifford, West Virginia's first African-American attorney and a civil rights pioneer in the early 20th century. I think the Post Office ought to consider many, many more lawyers. Doesn't anyone on O.J. Simpson's dream team qualify?

Inventors are another story. Just about every inventor you can think of has his or her own stamp. Some of the 22 inventors I haven't heard of, like William Dickson, a motion picture camera inventor, John Ericsson, a Swedish inventor of steam engines and distance finders, and Jan Ernst Matzeliger, the inventor of the lasting machine that attaches a shoe upper to the sole 15 times faster than a skilled human can do it.

I didn't see any broadcast essayists on the list of postage stamps, but I can't imagine a more appropriate category. H.L. Mencken, Andy Rooney, and Mark Levy would be a good start, in my humble opinion.

Surprise!

P eople love surprises. Well, not all people, of course. But enough people love them that the paper gift wrapping industry is bigger than ever. There's nothing quite like opening a present that's encased in wrapping paper. Birthdays, anniversaries, Christmas, pink slips... almost everything seems to be appreciated more when it's wrapped in colorful paper.

Frankly, I'm one of the people who don't like surprises. I'm just as happy and excited to receive a big check, for example, whether it's concealed in an envelope or just plain naked.

Ditto for a book I'm anxious to read. Imagine how difficult it would be if every book in a bookstore were packaged in wrapping paper. Maybe that's the way they are displayed and sold in an alternate universe, but it sure doesn't make a lot of sense, does it?

I think part of the reason I don't like surprise presents is because I, myself, can't wrap them very well. That seems to be a more common problem among men than women, for some reason. A recent survey indicates that 71 percent of us believe that women are better gift wrappers than men. And 74 percent of us say that the female head of household is most likely to wrap the majority of holiday gifts in their home.

Hallmark, the company that introduced modern gift wrapping in 1917, says the gift wrap industry accounts for $3.2 billion a year in retail sales. Now that's a statistic it's difficult to wrap my head around.

One of the most important decisions a couple has is whether to have a baby. And the big guessing game related to that decision is what the gender of your unborn baby is. People are divided into two groups: those who want to know in advance and those who want to be surprised.

Some people are superstitious about knowing the baby's gender before he or she is born. I don't know what they think will happen if they find out in advance of the birth, but I'm sort of afraid to ask. Of course, a thousand other traits of the baby are not known until it's born, like eye color, length of eyelashes, skin shade, musical aptitude, and desire to be a vegetarian. Someday, we might be able to know all those traits in advance and I'll be the first one on line to inspect the report.

Even people who want to know their baby's sex usually don't obsess over those other traits. They are generally complacent not to know every detail. But the gender of the baby... well, that's another thing. They can't wait to find out. For those who want to be surprised at the last minute, maybe nurses and doctors in the delivery room can be trained to giftwrap the kid before presenting it to the mother. That would be the logical next step, I think, in the whole baby producing business. Remember: you heard it here.

Here's another area that is more predictable than it used to be: weather forecasting. Everyone seems to want to know what the weather will be like in the near and far future. A couple of hundred years ago, tomorrow's weather was often a surprise. But weather predicting has come a long way since Noah and his Ark. I don't know anyone who wants to be surprised in the morning, if he can help it. And goodness knows, the preoccupation with tomorrow's or next week's weather is catered to by television news shows that bombard us with predictions — sometimes accurate ones — four or five times during each nightly broadcast.

Another area in my life in which I don't like to be surprised, especially distastefully surprised, is food at a restaurant. There's nothing worse than spending a fair amount of money on a meal that's inedible or, as my daughters used to say, gross. That's why I never order chili in a new restaurant. Since so many recipes for chili are available, it means chili from the joint I visit can be a major disappointment. It's better to make chili myself, so I know in advance, more or less, what it's going to taste like. I guess I can say the same for, say, chocolate ice cream, but it's really chili that causes me the most angst.

When I do cook for myself or others, I don't taste the food or peek in the oven before it's done, even though professional chefs advise cooks to do that. What can I tell you? That's the exception to my general rule. I like to surprise myself with my own cooking.

The bottom line is, so many things are unpredictable in life, eliminating as many surprises as possible seems smart.

The Fuzz That Was

I can't say that having Matt, my barber, shave my head for the first time was a relief, even though I'd been discussing the possibility for months and agonizing over the consequences for weeks.

The mere thought of removing my precious score of hair strands from the top of my head caused foreboding. How would I deal with taking that traumatic step beyond the point of no return? How could I face my family, friends, and business associates? I was apprehensive about their reactions to this sudden and drastic change of appearance.

However illogically, I blame the U.S. Air Force for my condition. In basic training, my luxurious, wavy, long, dark brown locks were unceremoniously removed in 30 seconds. In the ensuing two decades, they never grew back, at least not entirely. What did remain at the periphery of my head was the subject of sound and frequent discussions, never ridicule, with my barber, Matt.

"Get yourself a hair blower," he advised in '86, demonstrating an under-brushing technique to fluff my hair.

"The secret of hair styling is form over substance."

He encouraged me to use conditioner. He trimmed my beard in an effort to misdirect the casual observer.

"Plastic brush bristles are no good," he declared. "They strip and damage your hair. After a while your hair will look lifeless. You need to protect the hair you have," he smiled, "since you can't afford to lose what you've got." Matt has a full head of hair, although he's older than I am. I guess we have a love/hate relationship.

I concentrated and remembered every word he said. A barber's advice is no laughing matter, although the end result of a hair cutting session may well be hilarious, as we all know.

Unfortunately, even after following Matt's advice assiduously every year, fewer and fewer strands of hair were available to camouflage my ever-expanding scalp. Ironically, my chest and back continued their tomentous course.

The topic of hairless heads, per se, has never been disconcerting to me. In fact, I'm often the first to enumerate the advantages of being bald:

1. First in a crowd to notice the onset of rain.
2. Easily recognized from any direction.
3. Huge savings in hair care products.

Despite the profusion of bald jokes, there's very little stigma in American society. In fact, some jokes actually extol the condition.

"God made just a few perfect heads…"

History and modern culture offer many examples of the attractive, the virile, or the notorious. More bald actors are on film lately and they don't always play villains. The villains don't always wear black hats either, nowadays; they merely smoke. Lately, we're exhibiting much less acceptance or even tolerance for men who wear cheap hair pieces or who comb their neck hair forward.

Baldness is positively prerequisite for national weather forecasters. Athletes in every sport are also strutting their scalpy stuff. We non-celebrities have changed, too. With the exception of rock concerts, hairless or partially hairless pates form a significant percentage of any audience. I know, because my cheap seats are always in the back of the auditorium or stadium.

I returned home after my memorable session with Matt. Frankly, it was an embarrassingly short session. But what did I expect for 16 hairs? And no, I didn't ask to take them home.

Late for dinner, as usual, I joined my wife and two teenaged daughters whose animated conversation was already in progress. I kept quiet for a few minutes, but the conversation failed to turn hirsute.

Finally, I blurted, "Notice anything different?"

They looked at me, expectantly. Both girls perused my features but neither one noticed The Change.

"It's my new doo," I whined.

They continued to stare quizzically. It was more than a little disillusioning, after all the nervous energy I'd expended, to find that my closest relatives could remain unaware and unimpressed.

In the following days, my colleagues also failed to notice the deforestation. My very best and most critical friends were equally oblivious. And that made an incident a few weeks later all the more gratifying for me. By then, at long last, I'd become reconciled to a simple fact: what I believed was a turning point in my life just didn't register on the Richter scale of human events.

I was at my mother's house for dinner.

"Shaved it off?" she observed off-handedly, serving soup.

"Oh, that," I replied quietly. "Thanks for noticing, Mom."

The Hats I Wear

I look darn good in hats. This isn't braggadocio; it's merely a factual observation.

When I try on a cowboy hat, I resemble John Wayne and [JOHN WAYNE ACCENT:] *it doesn't hurt to tell ya, pardner, get off ya horse and drink ya milk.*

When the cowboy hat is black, with authority I can say, [JOHNNY CASH ACCENT:] *"Hello, I'm Johnny Cash."*

I can wear a beret, and [FRENCH ACCENT:] *you could tell zhat I am zee artist, Français.*

[BRITISH ACCENT:] *A jaunty bowler makes me appear decidedly British.*

With a suitably floppy sombrero, I look as Mexican as Anthony Quinn.

And though I have not attempted to make a turban, [EAST INDIAN ACCENT:] *I vould be very happy to mess with toes New York Indian cab drivers.*

When you're bald, you see, any hat is an improvement. I used to say I have a bald spot, but I'm way beyond that now. I know what they say about certain bald men looking sexy, but I never feel as sexy as when I've got a nice cap to adorn the human bowling ball I call my head.

A hat is about the only artifice — if I can call it that — that is acceptable in modern society. Wigs or toupees are almost always noticeable and often the subject of ridicule. Hair plugs and Rogaine rarely work as well as their TV commercials promise. The somewhat popular comb-over doesn't fool anyone.

Besides, the wearer must always stand perpendicular to the prevailing wind. A sudden breeze or a child's friendly mussing can be deadly.

I haven't found shoe polish that's exactly the color of my remaining strands of hair.

No, only a hat is a socially acceptable solution, nowadays, to a bald man's dilemma.

As I mentioned, donning the appropriate dialect and accent, as well as believable demeanor, is essential. If you can't pull off the accent, it's better not to say anything. Whatever you do, please try not to sound like a bald guy.

The Last Supper

In the movie, *Annie Hall*, Woody Allen tells an old joke: two old women were complaining about a restaurant. One said, "the food is terrible," and the other replied, "yes, and the portions are too small."

The other day, I was bemoaning the state of air travel with my nephew, who's traveled a lot more and for longer distances than I have. But that's not saying much, as I hate to travel. I've been out of this country only a handful of times, if you count New Jersey.

The topic with my nephew got around to food, as my conversations are apt to do.

In the distant past, airline food had developed a reputation of being pretty bad with the portions being too small, just like the *Annie Hall* women said. But when airlines stopped serving meals, people complained. I was one of them.

Just about the time the airlines were cutting back on food service, however, the airports themselves started attracting more and higher end retail food establishments. Now, the major airports offer restaurants that serve everything from pizza and ice cream to fine steak dinners.

My nephew confided to me that he liked to get to airports early or arrange for longer layovers, so he could sit down for an excellent meal before or between flights.

"I believe in having a sumptuous meal before a flight," he said. "I pull out all the stops and order the most luxurious meal on the menu of the best restaurant in the airport, have a glass or maybe a bottle of expensive wine, a fancy appetizer, and a decadent dessert. Not only will I not get hungry on the flight, but let's face it, the plane may go down before its scheduled landing and the meal I have at the airport could be my last one."

That conversation with my nephew actually made a lot of sense. What's the price of a good meal compared to the price of an airplane ticket? Now, instead of complaining about airline food, I look forward to having a great meal at the airport. In fact, I can hardly wait to take another trip.

The Pleasures of Psoriasis

I've got good news to share today. I think I have a spot of psoriasis.

It's just a little spot on my left forearm, but it's enough for me to feel pretty good. I'll tell you why in a few minutes. But first, let me tell you what I found out about the disease. In general, psoriasis causes pain, itching and joint stiffness. There are 5 major types of psoriasis. Psoriasis vulgaris -- also known as chronic, stationary psoriasis or plaque-like psoriasis -- is the most common form and affects about 90% of people with psoriasis. Plaque psoriasis typically appears as raised areas of inflamed skin. Itchy, painful lesions are called "plaques" and usually occur on the lower back, elbows, knees and scalp. Then there's guttate psoriasis. The lesions that appear with guttate psoriasis look more like small red dots. The third type is inverse psoriasis, which occurs when lesions look like large red blotches and usually occur in the groin, armpit or behind the knee. Next comes pustular psoriasis, raised patches of white blood cells that can occur anywhere on the body. Finally, erythrodermic psoriasis affects only 3% of psoriasis sufferers, so I won't bother to gross you out about it.

"What causes psoriasis?" you might ask. Doctors think that psoriasis is a condition that gets triggered by something else. Scientists have identified more than 25 genes that may be responsible for causing and/or triggering psoriasis. Turns out, stress is a known trigger. Believe it or not, certain "traditional" stress remedies like smoking cigarettes, drinking alcohol, and using drugs can actually make psoriasis worse. It's an upside-down world. So just calm down, give up all your pleasures, and you may not get a psoriasis flare-up. That's my advice.

No two cases of psoriasis ever look exactly alike, which doesn't make diagnosis easy. But in my case, I'm pretty sure I've got it.

Or it might be eczema.

According to the WebMD site, eczema causes an intense itch. It can get so bad that you scratch enough to make your skin bleed. Psoriasis, on the other hand, could also be itchy, but your skin may sting or burn, like you're getting bitten by fire ants.

Actually, for me it's none of the above... no itching and no stinging and the spot is on my arm, not my back, my elbows, or my groin. But regardless of those minor details, I know what I know.

"Okay, how do we treat or cure psoriasis?" you ask. There's topical treatment, which can ease itching and pain. Topical, of course, is just a fancy word for something you put on your skin. Topical vitamin D, selenium, fish oil, and vitamin B12 might work, but then again they might not.

Then there's oral treatment, which focusses on inhibiting inflammation that leads to psoriatic flare-ups. There's also systemic, or "whole body" treatment to treat the body's immune system function. We also have biologic treatment, which are injectables based on human gene proteins. Did I mention that at least 25 genes may be responsible for causing psoriasis? Good luck finding and nullifying the right ones.

Doctors have also attempted to use ultraviolet light therapy to reduce psoriasis flare-ups. And, last but not least, there are alternative treatments that include herbs, acupuncture, tai chi, yoga, meditation, etc. You know the routine. Needless to say, not everything works for everybody. In fact, most of these treatments don't seem to work for anybody, which is why the pharmaceutical companies keep introducing new pills, ointments, and lotions.

Some doctors think being overweight isn't a good idea, so they recommend reducing caloric intake. The good news is, these doctors say a hypocaloric diet is the way to go. You should lose weight only by consuming a smaller number of calories, rather than by exercise or surgery. Frankly, that sounds a lot easier than spending every free moment on a treadmill. But maybe that's just me.

To reduce inflamed areas, many doctors say you're not supposed to even look at processed foods, refined sugars, fatty cuts of red meat, or dairy, all of which make your inflammation worse, even if it makes your life more interesting.

Now I can tell you why I'm so happy to have discovered a bit of psoriasis on my arm. I can finally relate to the TV commercials that advertise biologics to control my body's immune response. For the first time, I feel the announcers of commercials are talking directly to me when they extol the supposed benefits of what I call the Big Seven meds: Humira, Enbrel, Aveeno, Taltz, Cosentyx, Stelara, and Otezla.

As for eczema treatments, I've found 154 of them, but sadly they'll have to wait for another day.

The fact that side effects from the Big Seven psoriasis treatments can be diarrhea, nausea, headache, and upper respiratory infection is a small price to pay for joining the cub of my fellow psoriasis sufferers, whatever and wherever they're scratching.

Unique Dog Names

You'll be relieved to know we've adopted a new puppy after losing our last one, who was an 8-pound, friendly Chihuahua named Cashew. Our new puppy is a cross between a sheep dog and a poodle. It's a sheepadoodle and we've named him Sherlock, after an obscure fictional detective who was known to wear a deerstalker. Can't wait for next Halloween, as you can imagine.

Anyway, choosing Sherlock's name was not hard, thanks to my sister's suggestion. But just for fun, I thought I'd see what other unique appellations people named their dogs.

Popular names were easy to Google. The Internet is full of dog names, sorted by hair color, breed, size, personality traits, or celebrities. As an example, I'll give you some dog names I found on one site called rover.com.

For male dog names, the most popular ones, in order, are Max, Charlie, Cooper, Buddy, Jack, Rocky, Duke, Bear, Tucker, and Oliver. Nothing particularly flashy about that list.

Female dog names, in order of popularity, are Bella, Lucy, Luna, Daisy, Lola, Sadie, Molly, Bailey, Maggie, and Stella.

Things got more interesting when I searched for the most unique dog names. Forgive the oxymoron, but the most popular unique dog names, in order, are Beau Dacious, Won Ton, Reeses Puppycups, Sitka, Lupin, Willie Nelson, Gryffindor, Artoo Dogtoo, Tater Tot, Tyrion, Hashtag, Tony

Romo, Sativa, Chronic, Espresso, Blade, Ernest Hemingway, Muttley Crue, Yeti, and WiFi.

One of the more complete sites for this sort of thing is petplace.com. For example, dozens of dog names are classified in petplace.com under personality types, like aggressive, cute or beautiful, fast, funny, loving, not so smart, ornery, and talkative. Sherlock doesn't talk, by the way. He just barks. Loudly and incessantly.

You can spend a lot of time surfing the Internet for dog names, but I don't advise it. After half an hour, I realized I made a mistake with Sherlock's name.

But it's too late now. My next project is to train little Sherlock to stop barking long enough to grip a calabash pipe between his teeth.

Upside-Down World

I know I can't be the first to notice that the world is upside-down. Let me show you what I mean.

Take Darwin's survival of the fittest theory. We learned that those most fit survived long enough to reproduce, so their genes could be passed down to future generations. That means the most beautiful birds, the fastest leopards and the strongest elephants were likely to propagate their genetic traits for generations.

But all of a sudden, along comes human civilization to change the rules. In centuries past, young men who were the healthiest and the strongest were the ones who survived. Nowadays, a healthy young person can be enlisted into military service. Depending upon which war or conflict he or she is sent to, that young person has a chance of not coming home, or at least not coming home in one piece. Instead, it's the young people with bad eyesight or heart arrhythmia or fallen arches who are spared the ordeal of battle, leaving those we would have called the "fittest" to risk their lives. So when it comes to war in modern times, it's the unhealthy among us who are the fittest and most likely to stay home and reproduce.

Here's another example of the upside-down world we call modern society. Just a few short years ago, those who talked to themselves were considered crazy. But now with iPods, cell phones, blue tooths and PDAs, it's those who are NOT talking or singing to themselves whom we're suspicious of.

"What's wrong with that guy standing by himself in the corner?" my wife asked the other day. "He's not grooving to some music or calling his friends. He's just standing there, looking anti-social. He gives me the creeps." Actually, it turned out to be Donald Trump, who was quietly adjusting his hair.

Here's one more example of the upside-down world we inhabit. My lovely wife has a heart of gold. When she sees something going awry, she's the first person to lend a hand. This seems to happen most often at restaurants. When we are attended by a waiter or waitress who serves us perfectly, my wife tips handsomely. But if the server happens to be inept, clumsy, forgetful or ill-tempered, my wife feels especially badly for the poor creature and over tips. The worse the server is, the more tip will be left. Granted, I don't know too many people with my wife's sense of fair play, thank goodness, but if more people were like my wife, more servers would be basket cases. We would see healthy, coordinated servers shipped to the front lines, leaving behind only the inept ones to wait on me.

Voting Age

In 1971, around the time of the Vietnam War, Congress proposed the 26th Amendment to the Constitution, lowering the voting age from 21 to 18. States ratified the proposal and it's now part of the Constitution. One argument for the Amendment was that a person who was old enough to fight for his country, and perhaps die for his country, should be allowed to vote. Sounded reasonable at the time, especially to the under-21 crowd.

Now, some teenagers are using a similar argument to try to convince the rest of us that 18 is old enough to drink their weight in the alcoholic beverage of their choice. But that's a subject that will wait for another time.

Actually, I just learned there's a movement afoot to lower the voting age again. Senator Steve Kelley, a Democrat from Hopkins, Minnesota, introduced a bill to allow 17-year-olds to vote.

I'll bet Senator Steve is a hot guy who can win re-election if enough 17-year-olds will vote for him. But that's just the beginning. Some activists want to lower the voting age to 16. They say that most 16-year-olds can work, pay taxes, drive, and be charged as adults for crimes — even be sentenced to death. Welcome to adulthood, kids.

Frankly, I agree we haven't gone far enough. Many of our laws apply equally to younger people and to AARP members. Shouldn't those young people have a voice in deciding which lawmakers should represent them?

After all, in New Hampshire, girls as young as 13 can marry, as long as they have permission from their parents.

That's what? Seventh grade? When I was that age, I still couldn't ride my bicycle without training wheels.

Consider environmental legislation. Don't young people breathe the same air and drink the same water, not to mention beer, as older people? These folks will be six years older (and so will we, come to think of it) by the time their newly-elected senator's term is close to ending. Shouldn't they be allowed to have a say in which senator's term will expire?

Of course, the right to reproductive freedom also comes to mind. If a 13-year-old is mature enough to choose a husband or, yes, to become pregnant, shouldn't she be considered mature enough to vote and to decide whether her state legislators, her congressional representatives, her judges, or her President will be pro-choice or pro-life?

William F. Buckley wanted to bring back the poll tax, since that would ensure that only serious, invested adults would vote if they had to pay for the privilege. But the 24th Amendment to the Constitution put an end to poll taxes in 1964. That's one more revenue stream cut off at the source, but who's counting?

My proposal to drop the voting age doesn't seem so outrageous, does it? After all, a lot of adults can't make the right choice at a salad bar. Yet they can vote for the leaders of our country, merely because they're old enough. It's like saying only senior citizens can eat prunes. Oh, bad example.

Let's face it: if we lowered the voting age to 13, immature kids wouldn't bother to vote anyway. I mean, we can't even get them to clean their room, much less perform their civic duty. There would be very little risk that the politicians we elected could be worse than most of the ones we have always had. Perhaps less jaded minds might be able to cut through campaign smokescreens better than the rest of us. What have we got to lose?

Hey, maybe we could register teenagers to vote at salad bars.

We Famous People

What do Pablo Picasso and the Waltz King, Johann Strauss have in common? Here's a hint: one out of 365 of us — that's about 800,000 in this country — should know. Right. Picasso and Strauss were born on the same day, and that day was October 25th. It also happens to be a day in 1929 between Black Thursday and Black Monday, when the Dow Jones Industrial Average fell 23% in two days.

So, one out of 365 of us — including Helen Reddy and me — were born on October 25th. On that day in 1948, the United Nations charter was one day old. I tell people that my birthday is easy to remember: it's the day after United Nations Day. For some reason, though, people don't seem to recall that. It's probably a subconscious block on the part of those who don't believe the U.N. can bring a lasting worldwide peace. What do they know?

I started a club once, open to all lawyers in my county born on October 25th. There were three of us. It was pretty active, as clubs go. We met at a restaurant for a drink every year on our birthday. Then one of our members died and we had to disband. The remaining two of us couldn't agree on a place to meet.

The Internet has made it easy to find people born or events that occurred on my birthday. A web site I like is brainyhistory.com. It lists all sorts of events — mostly insignificant — that occurred on various October 25ths. For instance, did you know that the comic strip, "Little Orphan

Annie" was first published on October 25, 1924? Now be honest. Do you care?

Finding out who was born on your birthday and what momentous events happened on your birthday are two more reasons to buy a computer. I just wish Helen Reddy would answer her email.

We Vote on Everything

I think we Americans have taken this voting thing too far. It's one thing to vote for our elected government officials, the way our Founding Fathers specified. And I don't object to voting on occasional propositions to express our opinion about spending money on certain capital improvements and school systems.

Doesn't voting for singing or dancing amateurs on TV demean the importance of voting? Last season's American Idol show had almost as many voters as turned out for our last Presidential election.

I'm a big fan of *The Jerry Springer Show*. But it disturbs my sensibilities when he asks us viewers to call in and express our opinion on, say, whether a defrocked priest should be able to date minor orphans. I just wonder why Jerry asks our opinion and what affect our opinion will have on the world, his show, or even defrocked priests.

Speaking of the effect of our opinions or polls or votes, I am most amused when natural and often unchangeable phenomena are voted on. Do you think global warming is taking place? Do you think our world's weather patterns really care what you or even all of us think? How about the price of oil? Do you think it's too high? You probably do. So what? Are too many teenaged girls getting pregnant? Let's vote. Take a poll. That could change everything. Or not.

What Winning the Lottery Doesn't Mean to Me

I am driving home Wednesday night with a New York State lottery ticket in my pocket, thinking about how my life will change when I win $10 million.

Most of us lottery players think about this topic, from time to time, especially in the moments when the numbers bounce into view from the wonderful plastic bingo ball dispenser on T.V. We think about paying off our bills, buying jewelry — the outrageously expensive gaudy kind — cars, ditto, and houses — many of them. We think of taking trips, always first class, to exotic places. The more altruistic of us, of course, contemplate paying for our children's education, or our parents' long-term health care. For the more generous among us, supporting one or more philanthropic causes is definitely on the list.

This evening, however, I think not about what I would do with an appreciable portion of a multi-million-dollar jackpot, but what I wouldn't.

From the grandiose to the trivial, I realize that my life is filled with things that can be eliminated by the possibility of independent wealth. Here are the things I intend to give up:

1. I would no long steam or peel off uncanceled postage stamps.

2. When dining out, I would no long agonize over the relative value of one appetizer over another on a dollars per ounce basis.

3. I would no longer deduct the tax from my restaurant bill before I calculate the tip.

4. I would no longer begrudge the hatcheck woman her tip.

5. I would no longer park my car five blocks away from the restaurant or hotel to avoid valet parking.

6. I would no longer walk across the street merely to avoid the street musician with his open guitar case obstructing the sidewalk.

7. If I won the lottery, I would no longer belong to any organization that required my presence at 8:00 o'clock or — shudder — earlier in the morning.

8. I would no longer compare supermarket prices of tuna fish or cereal.

9. I would no longer purchase supermarket flowers.

10. I would no longer wait for my favorite brand of soda to go on sale or settle for a generic brand.

11. I would no longer buy the economy size of anything that tends to get soggy, go flat, or smell yucky towards the end of its life.

12. With respect to open milk containers, I would no longer resolve doubt in favor of freshness.

13. If I were a millionaire, I would no longer scrape the sides of peanut butter jars.

14. I would no longer precariously drain ketchup from one bottle to another.

15. I would no longer scoop melons down to the rind.

16. I would no longer drink tap water.

17. I would no longer eat leftovers. Come to think of it, I would no longer place leftovers in my refrigerator. In fact, I would no longer have need for plastic wrap or aluminum foil.

18. I would no longer put up with dull knives, dull scissors, or dull people at cocktail parties.

19. I would no long borrow my neighbor's snow blower. In fact, I would no longer personally remove snow from my driveway or anyone else's or even my walkway.

20. I would no longer buy seats in the bleachers.

21. If I were independently wealthy, I would no longer be tempted to purchase a monstrously large popcorn and drink at the movies merely because it's the best value.

22. I would never see the inside of store whose last four letters were M-A-R-T.

23. I would no longer buy my clothing out of season.

24. I would no longer wear jeans with holes in them unless fashion designers made it clear that they looked the coolest that way.

25. I would no longer check my watch before I began a long-distance call and every minute thereafter. For that matter, I would no longer even wear a watch.

26. I would no longer fill up with the lowest grade of gasoline and I would never again pump gas myself.

27. I would no longer keep toll receipts.

28. I would no longer keep a list of books to watch for a year after publication when they are scheduled to come out in paperback.

29. I would no longer reuse mouse traps.

And finally,

30. I would no longer open any envelope on which Ed McMahon's face appeared.

When Will You Die?

O f all the days in the year, on which day are you most likely to die? Stay tuned. The answer is coming up.

Before I researched this bit of trivia, I would have thought you could get a turkey bone stuck in your throat at a Thanksgiving dinner or you might be standing too close to a powerful fireworks display on the Fourth of July. Perhaps, I would have thought, you might be run over by an inebriated celebrant on New Year's Eve. You might be overwhelmed with emotion on the anniversary of your wedding. Or you might have a cardiac arrest when an irate husband comes crashing through a motel door while you're entertaining his wife.

But no. Statistically, the day you're most likely to die is your birthday. A study of 25 million dead people indicates that your chance of dying on your birthday is 6.7% higher than what you'd otherwise normally expect on that day. And when your birthday falls on a weekend some year, your chances are slightly higher.

Deaths, of course, can be due to a number of causes. Suicides and falls happen much more often on people's birthday and you can expect a 14% higher probability of death by strokes and heart attacks if you're more than 60 years old.

I found a wonderful, if not gruesome web site that tells you what activities are most likely to kill you. For example, only one in a million people die while swimming, which is about the same for runners and joggers, but base jumpers – you know, people who jump off buildings, for example – die at the rate of one in 60. If you climb a mountain in the Himalayas over three miles high, you'll have a solid 10% chance of not getting back alive. In general, your probability of dying during a given year doubles every eight years.

Table games and chess are pretty safe. Only one in 100 million players will die next year, presumably when they hear the pronouncement, "check mate." The web site is www.besthealthdegrees.com/health-risks.

I don't know about you, but I'm planning to stay in bed all day on my next happy birthday. What can possibly go wrong?

Women are Irrational - That's All There is to That

A bout two dozen people make my host's living room cozy. At any given time, six or eight cacophonous conversations are underway. And just like a dance in the junior high school gym, the men cluster on one side of the room, isolated from the women on the other.

A short time after arriving, I experience a foreboding sense that doing ANYTHING else would be more productive, more fulfilling, more fun. The event is so boring, I realize, because I spend the evening with the guys. You see, simply put, I prefer the company of bright women.

Flying in the face of political correctness, as I frequently do, daring to suggest that differences may exist between genders, I find myself landing on fragile, shifting ground. The fact is, however, that certain differences do exist between men and women — differences both physical and cognitive. So much for political correctness.

The average "rational" conversation of a group of men tends to pertain to sports, politics, business, or cars. Occasionally, an anecdote about the weather may blow in, but this is short-lived, since there is rarely an opportunity on that subject for guys to boast, brag, or bluster. Somehow, we always seem to get back to sports.

It may be congenital, but the subject bores me. Truthfully, it's beyond boredom. For me, it's absolutely mind-numbing. I am bewildered by the number of sports there are, the number of teams, divisions, and leagues, and the number of players. For the life of me, I can't distinguish Davis' cup from Stanley's. I don't know if Magic Jordan is a rock star or a sneaker. It's hopeless.

I have no affinity for soccer, no patience for baseball, and not the vaguest appreciation of hockey's offside rule. Even in tennis and football — sports I used to play as a teenager — I can't discuss a game or an athlete for more than thirty seconds. It seems so superficial. You can appreciate why my contribution to sports conversations is seldom more than a sympathetic smirk or a stifled yawn.

But it's not merely avoiding men's conversations that drives me to seek the company of women at social events. I have positive reasons, too. My conversations with women are inevitably relaxed, quite often substantive and interesting, and sometimes downright provocative. The subject matter has spanned such topics as Zen philosophy, art, sex, cooking, travel, child rearing, technology, ethics, education, the occult, surgical procedures, literature, movies, penile implants, organized religion, restaurants, music, TV, animal behavior, old age, and flying saucers.

From the esoteric to the latest gossip, women partners in conversation can most often be counted on to provide an animated and memorable intellectual experience. I'm not sure why this is. It might be because of the unpredictability of their discussions. Or it might be due to their openness to consider diverse and unconventional issues — a willingness that is a function of right-brain, intuitive thinking and liberal, accepting attitudes that I don't find in most of my male acquaintances.

Whatever the reason, and for want of a better explanation of the phenomenon, I can't help thinking that, in general, intelligent women are irrational, that's all there is to that Irrational in the finest, most inspiring sense of the word.

It certainly makes for a more enlightened and lively evening of conversation.

Sometimes, I wonder how such women could possibly be interested in men. What do they see in us? I'll have to ask a group of them at the next cocktail party.

Zen and the Art of Downhill Skiing

A few seasons ago, it happened: Lisa, my 10-year-old, beat me down the mountain at our favorite ski resort. As I peered through the powder that she kicked up and saw her come to a screeching halt at the lift line, I realized that I was out of excuses. I couldn't very well say that I was not prepared for the race. After all, it was my idea. Nor could I say that my equipment was outdated. Nothing was wrong with my legs or my feet or my back. In fact, I was feeling pretty good and I never skied faster in my life.

My little girl simply beat me, fair and square.

When Lisa and I arrived at the ski resort that fateful Sunday, we took the steps that everyone takes when they go skiing, culminating in standing at the end of a very long line.

And we waited. On an average weekend day, we could expect to spend about two hours skiing and six hours waiting on lift lines and riding chairlifts.

Finally our turn had come. The chair arrived and we took the long ride eventually making it to the top of the mountain.

We dismounted the chairlift and, as agreed, skied without stopping as fast as we could. When I caught up to Lisa, her first words were, "I beat you, Daddy."

"Oh," I wheezed, "were we racing?"

Waiting on the lift line once again, we heard people bragging to one another about their recent runs and their athletic prowess on the slopes. Others on the line complained about how long the line was and still others grumbled about how short were the runs.

Here I was, defeated by my 10-year-old, in the midst of a group of people complaining about the lift line and bragging about their abilities. I had gone skiing to relax, to ease the tension and stress built up over the previous week.

Competing at a ski resort with my daughter and overhearing petty verbal contests on the lift line had a mitigating effect on my goal of eliminating tension.

If the runs are so short and the lift lines are so intolerable, I began to wonder, why do we rush down the mountain to get back on the long line again?

I think in this case, the Japanese may have a better philosophy. Zen has been juxtaposed with many western phenomena, from business to motorcycle maintenance. But I don't believe it was ever been applied to downhill skiing.

The goal of Zen is to reach a harmonious and enlightened state of awareness. The philosophy is extremely easy to apply. The result is a wave of unexpected calmness and a feeling of peace and completeness and of being one with nature.

On the next chairlift up to the top, sitting next to my victorious daughter, I closed my eyes and breathed slowly, rhythmically. I began to transcend to a different plane of consciousness. I became aware of machinery behind the chairlift, hearing and feeling the mechanical grinding, squeaking and rumbling of gears and pulleys.

At the top of the mountain, instead of whizzing down the hill, oblivious to everything but moguls, I began to attain a sense of harmony with my soul. I glided down the mountain ever so slowly, s-l-o-w-l-y, almost imperceptibly, at the rate of only feet or even inches per minute. Taking wide, wide turns, thoroughly inspecting the branches of the trees from all angles, noticing the way snow clings to pine needles, hearing and feeling the crunching and sliding of skies on snow. Experiencing the sensation of wind as it rustled through the trees and puffed against my body, seeing the effect of evergreens against the blue sky and the lovely and graceful balancing of branches.

Attention to the details of a microcosm leads to a greater understanding of the macrocosm. As you take the time to perceive nature as it unfolds ever so slowly while you creep down the mountain, then tranquility shall overtake you.

The day I discovered how the Zen philosophy could be applied to downhill skiing, Lisa had completed six runs in the time it took me to reach the bottom.

Time had slowed down, and for me that was a unique experience, better than almost anything I could imagine except, of course, the feeling I would have had if I had won the race with my daughter.

Acknowledgements

I owe a great debt to my Wilkes University creative writing cohort and to all the friends, teachers, writers, and editors who guided and encouraged me along the way. Or at least didn't discourage me.

My mother taught me to use keyboards — piano and typewriter. My father taught me many lessons in life, including how to use a slide rule. Now that I think of it, slide rules and typewriters are obsolete artifacts of a generation or more ago. Nevertheless I still love my parents and appreciate their wisdom more every day. And when slide rules come back into fashion, I'll appreciate them even more.

Jan Quackenbush, the leader of my first creative writing group, suggested I attend graduate school even at my advanced age. Prudy Taylor Board, the leader of my Florida writing group, is never at a loss for constructive comments and, in fact, is the principal reason these essays are seeing print. Of course, all the members of both writing group help sharpen my focus, too. And "Sagebrush Bob" Conrad, an inspiration to so many in the broadcasting field, gave me a chance to voice my observations over the airwaves.

My incredibly patient friend and fellow Sherlockian, Randall Stock, designed my web site and led me to believe I did it all myself. See for yourself. Here's the domain name: www.trophyenvy.net.

About the Author

Mark Levy is a member of the bar in New York, Florida, and Colorado and holds both a Bachelor's degree in physics and a Master of Arts degree in creative writing. As a member of the Baker Street Irregulars and Mensa, the high IQ society, Mark has interests above and beyond the area of intellectual property law in which he has practiced for 40 years: patents and trademarks. His first book, Trophy Envy (As Heard on the Public Radio Show "Weekend Radio") was released in 2019. Visit him at www.trophyenvy.net

Belanger Books

Made in the USA
Columbia, SC
22 November 2019